Faith Breaks, Volume 2
More Thoughts on Making It a Good Day

J. Howard Olds

WordStream Publishing, LLC
Nashville, Tennessee

Copyright ©2012 by the estate of J. Howard Olds

All rights reserved. Written permission must be secured from the publisher to use or reproduce any part of this book, except for brief quotations in critical reviews or articles.

Edited by: Jan Knight and April Benson

ISBN-13: 9781935758129 (paperback)/ 9781935758006 (eBook)

Printed in the United States of America

1 2 3 4 5 6 7 8 9 10

Faith Breaks Volume 2 is dedicated to my mother,
Edith Rose Stewart Lewis.
She was Owen County 2010 Mother of the Year
and models tenacity and faith on a daily basis,
no matter what. —Sandy Olds

Contents

Acknowledgements vii
Foreword ix

Attitude.. 1
Communication 14
Community 23
December 34
Easter People 46
Faith, Hope, & Love 52
Family 67
Gratitude 79
God in Our Lives 88
Our Nation 99
Peace 107
Prayer 118
Purpose 131
Time 146

Acknowledgements

As a second *Faith Breaks* book becomes a reality I am reminded of all those who have made this journey possible. Ann Carter in Crestwood, KY saw the value of these little radio spots so many years ago, and spent time reading and organizing the files. Since then, lots of other church member friends have been part of the process, but it was our dentist, Dr. Jack Fletcher in Brentwood, TN, who proposed printing a book of *Faith Breaks* and then went to work gathering friends to fund that first adventure. Thank you Brentwood United Methodist Church for your enduring support!

To begin, I want to thank my friend Jan Knight for her enthusiastic agreement to serve as the development editor for *Faith Breaks, Volume 2: More Thoughts on Making It a Good Day*. Prior to her retirement, Jan worked many years as Editor of *Pockets* magazine at The Upper Room in Nashville. It was a time-consuming task for her to read hundreds of Howard's scripts, and then select and organize 150 of them into chapters. Then, with her creative talent and a keen eye, April Benson served as content and copy editor to complete the final editing and polish the manuscript. Her dedication to the project was truly a gift!

I am also grateful to Dr. Frank Grisham for his encouragement and countless hours of work on the website **www.faithbreaks.org**. The website will be invaluable in inspiring and educating both laity and clergy through the publications of Howard's words. I have been left with a treasure of words written by one of the most effective communicators of the Gospel of Jesus Christ, and it is my vision to share that treasure.

My sons support and encourage me every step of the way. I appreciate their willingness to write the foreword to this volume and share their perspective on their dad and his ministry.

Thank you, Marti Williams, for seeing the value of bringing Howard's words out of the office files and into the hands of our beloved readers.

Finally, thank you, Readers, for taking time for a Faith Break.

— *Sandy Olds, 2012*

Dr. J. Howard Olds with his sons Brad and Wes

Foreword

"**Y**ou must be Howard's boy!"

We have heard this phrase throughout our lives whenever we would mention our last name. As soon as we said we were "Wes Olds" or "Brad Olds," many people would immediately connect our name to "Howard Olds." At times while growing up, the constant drumbeat of the ensuing conversation became somewhat annoying. It is, for example, hard to misbehave in school when every teacher already knows who your dad is on the first day of class! Even though the "boys" are now a forty-one-year-old Methodist Minister (Wes) and thirty-seven-year-old medical doctor (Brad), being known as "Howard's boys" is an honor.

J. Howard Olds was, indeed, well known in the communities we grew up in throughout Central Kentucky. Dad saw his role as pastor extending from the large congregations he served to the community at large. Long after we left home, he and Mom moved to Brentwood, Tennessee, where he served as senior pastor of a church with seven thousand members, Brentwood United Methodist Church. His life is an amazing story to us, especially when we consider his humble beginnings.

Raised in rural Owen County, Kentucky, God empowered Dad to touch hearts and transform lives in ways that even he found surprising. His childhood home was a small four-room house with no indoor plumbing whose previous residents included chickens, farm dogs, and cats. The work was hard, and the family scraped by. The local church he attended was far from the "megachurch" he would someday lead, yet the Gospel of Jesus was faithfully proclaimed from that pulpit, and our dad responded. And as the Apostle Paul would write about his own life, God's "grace was not without effect" in Dad's life.

Over the next forty-plus years, God moved him from a simple adolescence—when he won awards for show cows as the president of Future Farmers of America—to influencing thousands of people and having dinner with the President of the United States of America! While still a child, God called Dad to be a preacher, and he often practiced preaching to empty chairs he set up in the living room. God gave him our mom, Sandy, to be his wife and partner in life and in ministry. Barely out of high school, Dad began serving as a student pastor at several small churches in Central Kentucky. He made a difference in those places, and the impact our dad had on people is still quite evident in our daily lives. Through emails, letters, phone calls, and chance encounters, many people continue to share their stories of his positive influence that had touched them. Dad was just as comfortable as a pastor and counselor to individuals as he was to large crowds. For example, we still encounter proud, loving couples who inform us that he performed their weddings, buried their loved ones, or helped them through some hard times.

By the time we were old enough to remember, we could see that Dad lived what he preached. That was the core of his ministry. As children, our family home was shared with children from the Kentucky Methodist Home. We became their family for holidays and summer breaks when they had nowhere else to go. As a volunteer firefighter and chaplain in Crestwood, Kentucky, Dad brought home the family who had just lost their home to fire on Christmas Eve. In Lexington, our family welcomed the teenage mother and newborn baby who stayed in our family home when she had nowhere else to go. Dad had a core belief in God, family, and community.

After his death from cancer in 2008, we received many letters of sympathy and gratitude. One such letter included the story of a woman recovering from a traumatic brain injury. "Your Dad offered spiritual support to my family all the days I was in a coma, and he was in the room when I finally came out of it," she wrote. She attended church shortly thereafter. "Sure, I was a sad sight to see, shaved head growing bristly hair, and an eye patch. I felt very ugly and out of place. But the sermon penetrated my soul."

Dr. Brad Olds once received a message that read: "It seems very strange for me to be sending you this email addressed to 'Dr. Olds.' I, of course, think of your Dad. My family and I were members of St. Paul United Methodist Church in Louisville, Kentucky, for eleven years. It was a great privilege for me to know your father. I count him among the finest people I have ever known. He was a tremendous spiritual influence and inspiration."

While in Lexington, Kentucky, at Trinity Hill United Methodist Church, Faith Breaks emerged as a radio ministry. We remember all the preparations that went into making each word available to such a large audience. We watched and admired as Dad worked so diligently on each word that could deliver an inspirational message to a distracted city commuter in only a few seconds. But the words and the voice delivering their messages worked! The congregation even contributed to the ministry by volunteering to cover election poll results for news media in exchange for airtime. It is this collective commitment that we are proud to continue in this release of *Faith Breaks, Volume 2: More Thoughts on Making It a Good Day.*

To us, however, "Dr. J. Howard Olds" was simply just "Dad." We were the first recipients of the Faith Breaks you hold in your hand. He was someone who told us he "loved us no matter what" and assured us as we ventured out in life that we could "always come home again." More importantly, he was a man we could learn from, wrestle with, argue against, and who would hold us steady in times of trials. He stood with us in celebration during our graduations and weddings and mourned with us as we each lost one of our own children too soon. When he told us about God being one "who would never leave us or forsake us," he lived it out in our lives when times were tough.

We are so thankful for the ways that he loved his grandkids, Caleb, Ella, and Carrie, who called him "Poppy" as he poured love into each of their lives. He once told us that his grandchildren were a reward for "not killing his own children!" We now laugh as we knew that meant us! Dad told us that "every child needs two fathers," one in Heaven who is perfect and one on earth who is not. Now that we are both dads ourselves, we know what he meant when he said that "every child needs roots and wings." We are grateful we were graced with both these things.

It was admittedly sometimes tough to grow up being identified as "Howard's boys." Yet today, we delight in hearing people say that to us. It is our prayer that our own children will know the richness of the legacy of grace entrusted to them.

— Wes & Brad Olds, "Howard's Boys"

Attitude

Our Paintbrush

Two farmers lived side by side. One farmer was always positive. The other was always negative. The positive farmer thanked God for rain that watered his crops. The negative farmer complained that the rain made his hay rot. The positive farmer rejoiced in the sunshine which made things grow. The negative farmer was sure the hot sun was causing his plants to wilt.

One day the two farmers went duck hunting. As they sat in a small boat, a big goose flew by. When the negative farmer shot the goose, the positive farmer said, "Look what my dog can do!" Sure enough, the dog jumped out of the boat, ran across the top of the water, brought back the goose, and dropped it in the boat. Beaming, the positive farmer said to his neighbor, "What did you think of that?"

Shaking his head, the negative farmer replied, "Just what I thought, your poor old dog doesn't even know how to swim."

Life reflects the color of our thoughts. Attitude is our paintbrush on the barn doors of life! Is your attitude positive or negative?

O God of many blessings, help us
to approach life with the right attitude,
supported by faith in your love, mercy, and grace.
May our hope outshine our disillusionment. Amen

Heart Transplant?

A businessman who survived a heart transplant for ten years reflected on the difference a new heart made in his life. He said, "A heart transplant gave me a new urgency about life. I have changed my priorities. If I'm going to stop and smell the roses, I do it now. I no longer put important things off until tomorrow.

"A heart transplant gave me new gratitude for life. I have learned how to say thanks. Thanks to the medical profession for their expertise. Thanks to family and friends for their support. And most of all, thanks to God for the gift of life. I now live a grateful life.

"A heart transplant gave me a closer relationship with God. When someone goes with you through the valley, you develop a special bond with that person. My God and I walked through the transplant together."

In what condition is your heart today? You may not need a physical transplant, but could you use an attitude adjustment?

*Dear God of yesterday, today, and tomorrow,
help us to see the places in our lives
where we need to change our attitudes.
Give us the desire, courage, and persistence
to make those changes. Amen.*

Duck

Ben Franklin paid a visit to Puritan preacher, Cotton Mather, so the story goes. When Mr. Franklin started to leave, he continued talking as he made his way to the door. That's when the Reverend Mather started shouting, "Stoop! Stoop!" Ben Franklin didn't understand, so he didn't stop talking until he banged his head on a low beam near the doorway.

Recalling that story years later, Ben Franklin concluded, "I have avoided a lot of misfortunes by not carrying my head too high."

A little humility goes a long way in the community of life. Humility, simply defined, is remembering we are the created and not the Creator. It is the determination to treat all people with dignity and respect. When you walk into a room, does your body communicate "here I am" or "how can I help?" When it comes to the core values of your life, do you seek to serve or to be served? Maybe we would all do better if we ducked our heads once in a while.

Dear Jesus, you taught us how to live
with humility and in service with others.
Help us to pattern our lives after yours. Amen.

Anyway

I stumbled into a thought the other day that I'd like to share with you. It goes something like this:

People are unreasonable, illogical, and self-centered. Love them anyway. If you are kind, people may accuse you of selfish, ulterior motives. Be kind anyway. The good you do today will be forgotten tomorrow. Be good anyway. Honesty and frankness will make you vulnerable. Be honest and frank anyway. What you spend years building may be destroyed overnight. Build anyway. People need help but may attack you if you try to help them. Help them anyway. In the final analysis, it's between you and God. It was never between you and them anyway.

Life is a matter of action, not reaction. If we wait for others to set our agenda and determine our destiny, we will find ourselves tossed about with numerous conflicts and continual doubts. So why not live by a higher power? Let our attitudes be motivated by love, stimulated by kindness, directed by generosity for the good of others and the glory of God.

God of mercy, direct our attitudes to be such that others benefit from our living.
May we love anyway, be kind anyway, be honest anyway, help anyway. Amen.

Humility

Legendary football coach Tom Landry was not happy with his team, which consistently danced, wiggled, and spiked the football after each touchdown. So, in the locker room after the game, the wise coach offered this advice: "From now on, I want you to act like you have been in the end zone before." I suspect a lot of us in the game of life could use that kind of advice.

People who are not used to victory have a need to flaunt it every time they get it. Insecure people who are still trying to prove themselves have a habit of calling attention to the smallest accomplishment. They are like children who walk for the first time and expect the applause of everyone in the room.

Wisdom and experience, however, temper our need to strut, brag, and celebrate at the expense of others. When you know you've got it, there is no need to flaunt it. I am amazed at the humility of the truly wise and the consideration expressed by the thoroughly experienced. They don't have to be the biggest, loudest, control freaks at the cocktail party. Their reputations speak louder than words.

Dear Savior,
you humbled yourself and walked among us.
May we take your humility upon ourselves
and serve others in your name. Amen.

Breaking Point

A fit of road rage on I-65 the other day sent one commuter to the hospital and another easygoing father of three to jail. It also tied up morning rush hour traffic for more than two hours.

Has America become a nation of angry, short-tempered people? From road rage to airplane rage, grocery-store rage, and violence at youth sports events, episodes of explosive anger seem to be happening with unprecedented frequency. Three-fourths of Americans believe such angry behavior is getting worse.

What is causing such dangerous, destructive behavior? There are probably no simple answers. We are certainly living more tension-packed lives. People talk on the cell phone, listen to the radio, and plan their day's activities while navigating through heavy traffic on their way to work. We are never quiet. We are seldom calm. Does every soul have a breaking point? Who of us, trained to let it all hang out, have the patience or the self-restraint to think before we react? Maybe it's time to take charge of our emotions.

*Parent God of grace, we are your children,
but we often let anger and simmering resentment
keep us from reflecting your nature.
Help us to model to the world
your love, grace, and compassion. Amen.*

Seize the Day

I keep these words of William Penn on a plaque in my home: "I expect to pass through this life but once. Therefore, if there be any kindness I can show, any good I can do, let me neither defer it nor neglect it, for I shall not pass this way again."

In our lives, there are daily opportunities to do good. Occasionally such opportunities are bold and newsworthy. Some volunteer rescues a child from a burning building. An employee aborts a bank robbery. Most often, good deeds are ordinary and unnoticed. Courtesy on the highway is a good thing. Friendliness at the mall is an admirable attribute. A life of gratitude radiates in a thousand ways to others we meet on the street.

Do you seize the day for good? A child needs a hug. A friend needs a pat on the back. A community needs caring people who are willing to put in more than they take out. Never miss an opportunity to do all the good you can in all the ways you can.

Dear Lord, let us radiate love by living lives of gratitude. Let us not miss opportunities to do good today. Help us remember that even the smallest kindness can make a difference in someone's day. Amen.

Competition or Compassion?

In what condition might your compassion be? Is that a fair question to ask? Day by day, we tune into the trauma of the world. There are more car bombs in Baghdad. The ravaged Gulf Coast is a long way from being rebuilt. Somebody robs a liquor store. Another baby starves to death. For a moment our minds are shocked by such suffering and our hearts are touched with grief.

Author Henri Nouwen says, however, that most of our concern is short-lived. "Competition, not compassion, is our main motivation." We have work to do, a future to forge, an identity to carve into the crevices of time. In order not to be overwhelmed by pain, we keep a safe distance from suffering.

Yet compassion is the ability to suffer with another. It is to enter into the heartbreak, the heartache, the despair, the disorientation that another feels. It is to be weak with the weak, vulnerable with the vulnerable, and powerless with the powerless. It is hard work, but it is healing work.

*Compassionate God, we must ask ourselves
if we are compassionate people.
Help us to be imitators of you,
for we are your beloved children. Amen.*

Happiness

Happiness is… Well, recent studies in psychology say it's definitely not money. Instead, money will buy you "a stingy, selfish outlook on life," says Kathleen Vohs, a University of Minnesota marketing professor who reported the study. In a series of nine experiments with college students, the researchers discovered that even subtle reminders of money caused people to be less generous, more self-reliant, and more demanding of others. "The mere presence of money changes people," said Ms. Vohs.

As we rush to purchase the things money can buy, let us beware of the things money cannot buy. Money can't buy us health. The storms of illness blow against the just and the unjust. Money can't buy us meaningful relationships. As George Strait says in his country song, "I've got a furnished house, a diamond ring, and a lonely, broken heart full of love, and I can't even give it away." Money can't buy us hope for tomorrow. Only God can give us that.

You have given us so much, generous God.
Help us to remember that our money
and all of our possessions belong to you.
May we have a generous spirit. Amen.

Take This Job and Love It!

I ran into this saying the other day, and I thought it worth passing along: "Many people quit looking for work when they find a job." I don't know who I'm quoting, but I am quite certain the words are true. Do you have a job, or does a job have you? What would it take for you to take your job and love it? Are you more apt to say "thank God, it's Friday," or "thank God, it's Monday"?

Oh, I know—work can be boring and mundane. It can be demanding and time consuming. I personally know ministers who are a bore to themselves and their congregations. I have encountered nurses who let you know they do not really want to care for you. I have also encountered dishwashers who make dishwashing divine service and waitresses who make customers feel like royalty.

So let's just admit it. Work satisfaction is largely a matter of attitude. A bright attitude can transform any job into meaningful service. And a bad attitude can turn great opportunity into daily drudgery. Have you discovered the difference?

Dear Lord, help us to see our work with new eyes.
May we find ways to serve others
even when our tasks seem monotonous and mundane.
And may we work as thankful people. Amen.

I Can't!

"I just can't!" Do you ever say that? I seem to hear it every day. I just can't stop eating. I just can't stop smoking. I just can't communicate. I just can't get my work done. Of course, as my mother used to say, "Can't never could do anything."

So the first step to a finer, more fruitful life is a change of attitude. We must change "I just can't" to "with God's help, I will" and then go for it with all the faith and hope of a winner. We can live a healthy life. We can develop communication skills. We can do an honest day's work for an honest day's pay. When we do the things we can, with the help that is available, we begin to feel better about ourselves and live more productive and healthier lives.

So let us not enslave ourselves to anything. We were not made to be slaves. We were created to be free—free from oppression, free from habits that hurt us, free to become all God created us to be. Life is made to be enjoyed, not endured. Time is given to be used, not abused. Habits are meant to help us, not hinder us. So, by the grace of God, turn your "I can't" into "I can" today.

Dear God, we are familiar with the Bible verse that says we can accomplish great things through Christ, who sustains us, but we forget to apply it in our lives. Turn our "I can't" into "I will with God's help." Amen.

Reverence

"The person who bows before nothing will someday be flattened by the weight of himself." Have you considered that? A sense of reverence is essential to life. A sense of wonder, awe, and praise frees us from the pit of greed, self-pity, and senseless activity.

What creates a sense of reverence for you? If it's not the twinkle of a star, is it God who is never far from anyone of us? T.S. Eliot once said, "And the wind shall say 'here were decent godless people: Their only monument the asphalt road and a thousand lost golf balls.'" Is that all there is?

There are reasons to be born save to consume the corn, eat the fish, and leave behind a dirty dish. There are people to love, an environment to save, a God to serve. People who get all wrapped up in themselves make very small packages. So look all around you, find someone in need. Look up above you, see God instead of greed. Lost in wonder, love and praise, discover a life beyond yourself.

When we become too full of
ourselves and the busyness of our lives,
let us remember to make a joyful noise to you, O Lord,
and to come to you in thanksgiving and praise.
Remind us, dear God, what things are really important
and help us to reorder our priorities. Amen.

Sign

A clock repair shop displayed this sign in the window: "If your grandfather needs oiling and adjusting, we still make house calls." As a grandfather, there are times I could use some oiling and adjusting. How about you?

The oil of forgiveness reduces friction. The oil of understanding eliminates hurt. The oil of love keeps us together. The oil of joy keeps us ticking. The oil of hope encourages us to try one more time. People need oiling.

People need adjusting. The demands of the day and pressures of the years can alter life's rhythm to the extent that we still tick, but not on time. We have not maintained the balance of work and rest, power and purpose, time and eternity. Major adjustments are needed to our timing.

If you could use some oiling and adjusting, remember the Master Designer of the universe still makes house calls.

O God, we pray as the psalmist prayed:
"Put false ways far from us;
and graciously teach us your law.
We have chosen the way of faithfulness,
and we cling to your decrees, O Lord." Amen.

Communication
(Words, Words, Words)

Four Minutes a Day

A troubled wife told her husband they needed to improve their communication. Her husband immediately acted on the matter. He went down to the community college and enrolled in a course on public speaking. At the heart of all human relations, and especially in the close quarters of family life, lies the challenge of effective communication. While communication is not automatic, it is attainable. And here are a few pointers to get you started.

One, lower your voice. The old proverb is right. A gentle answer turns away wrath. Two, stop the blame game. Judge not that you be not judged. Three, speak the truth in love. Honesty continues to be the best policy. And finally, listen carefully. We were made with two ears and one mouth, so let that be a principle of our communication.

It's been estimated that typical U.S. married couples spend an average of four minutes a day in meaningful conversation. For the sake of ourselves and others, we can do better than that.

Dear God, prompt me to take time
to listen to family and friends.
And when I do, may my response
be gentle, honest, loving, and non-judgmental. Amen.

Out of Control

A friend sent me an e-mail with a list of signs that my life may be getting out of control. On the list were these things: "You have fifteen phone numbers to reach your family of three. Your daughter sells her Girl Scout cookies on the internet. You chat with a stranger from South Africa several times a week, but have not spoken to your neighbor this year. Your grandmother clogs up your e-mail inbox, asking for pictures of your newborn son."

Technology—we wonder how we ever lived without it? Now we wonder how to live with it. The very things that revolutionized communication now threaten to destroy communication between a husband and wife, a parent and child, neighbors in the same subdivision.

So why not be really revolutionary? Choose a day to shut down the computer. Turn off the TV. Put the cell phone on recharge, and get in touch with the people who matter in your life. Talk. Listen. Play. Pray. For people who need people are truly the luckiest people in the world.

You, O God, are always available to listen to us.
So let us not forget the people in our lives
who need our loving attention,
whether that attention be in the form of
conversing, listening, playing, or praying.
Help us to be present for them. Amen.

Our Wordy World

Words, words, words, words—we are daily inundated by a torrent of words. Words are softly whispered, lovingly proclaimed, or angrily screamed. Words are heard on radio, recorded on CDs, written in books, even strung through the sky. Words are the floor, the wall, the ceiling of our very existence.

In our wordy world, I sometimes wonder if we are saying anything or just drowning the sounds of silence. As a public speaker, I know there is a great deal of difference between having something to say and having to say something. Cable TV and talk radio have put broadcasters in the same predicament. E-mails written in the anger and loneliness of the night seem to have a vicious edge that would probably go unspoken in the light of day. Are we a better, kinder, gentler, nation as a result of this information revolution? Or have we become more vicious, obnoxious, and outright hateful with this convenience of communication?

The right word at the right time spoken in the right way to the right person for the right reason can do a world of good. Otherwise we will do well to keep quiet.

Let the words of our mouths
and the meditations of our hearts,
be acceptable in to you, O God.
May we speak the right words at the right times
or not at all. Amen.

Thumbs

I sprained my thumb the other day and got a free lesson on the intricate interaction of the human anatomy. With a sprained thumb, I found it difficult to pick up a tiny pin, tie a shoe, or write a note. Even eating proved to be a pain. It reminded me of the words of an ancient psalmist who exclaimed, "We are awesomely and wonderfully made."

A thumbprint establishes my unique identity. I twiddle my thumbs when I am bored. A thumbs up is a strong word of encouragement that never requires a single syllable of speech. Hitchhikers travel by thumbing their way to their desired destination.

If my thumbs speak louder than words, I wonder what the rest of my body is communicating? Do I walk into a room with arrogance or anticipation? Do I enter a conversation to learn or dispense advice? Do I sit through meetings bored? Do I communicate interest and concern? Well, the questions could go on, but you get the point. What is your body language communicating?

Dear Jesus, you said that whatever we do to others we do to you. Help us to meet and respond to people the same way we would if we were meeting and responding to you, because, in fact, we are. Amen.

Gossip

Gossip is a parasite that piggybacks onto people's need to be important, noticed and "in the know." Are you aware of that? Gossip is one of the most damaging things we do to others. It topples governments and wrecks marriages. It ruins careers, spawns suspicion, and generates grief. Gossip—it maims without killing. It breaks hearts and ruins lives. Gossip—the more it's quoted, the more it's believed. Politicians spread it. Television producers love to tantalize viewers with it. Ordinary people communicate it around card tables and coffee tables. No one knows what pain is caused by one person saying to another, "I don't know if it's true, but I just heard the most alarming thing about…" Such conversation should cause caring people to cover their ears, shut their mouths, and pray for mercy.

That's why one thoughtful person offers this prayer to begin each day. "O Lord, help my words be gracious and tender today, for tomorrow I may have to eat them."

*Dear God, let us not use our tongues to both bless you
and then harm those whom you
have created in your own image.
May your love for all of your children
be reflected in our words. Amen.*

Discretion

"For everything there is a season and a time for every purpose under heaven. There is a time to speak and a time to be silent." Those wise words from the writer of Ecclesiastes still ring true today. Have you the wisdom to know when to speak and when to be silent? We live in a verbal world. Everything talks to us—TVs, cell phones, cars, computers, radios, IPods. Well, the list goes on. We have become a people who speak our minds, say that we think, let our views be known. If telling secrets were the same as confession, our whole society would be on a confession binge. We are people who let it all hang out!

Let us not be fooled. A lot of verbiage is not synonymous with wisdom. Every thought does not merit expression. Every opinion is not worthy of consideration. Saying everything in the name of directness and honesty is not always the best way to communicate with others. Speech calls for discretion. There is a time to speak and time to be silent. Wise are those who know the difference.

O wise and all-knowing Lord,
help us to be wise in choosing our words
and in knowing when and how to use them.
May we not confuse verbiage with wisdom. Amen.

Making a Point

As Vicki Edwards has written on *Preaching Today's* website, "It's nice to talk with people who can make a point without impaling anyone on it." Have you thought about that? Most of us are intense about making a point. So we sharpen our opinions on the whetstone of polls and drown our audiences in statistics. We drive our truth home on the wheels of passion and round up the skeptics by persuasion. We preach with authority, speak with conviction, live with intensity. We know how to make a point.

But here's the question. Who is being impaled on the points we make? Who feels stabbed in the back, pierced in the side, slapped on the cheek by our comments? Are our words couched in anger or love, rage or respect, condemnation or compassion? The way we say things does make a difference.

Effective communication is always a challenge. That's true in community, in business, in families, and in churches. So let's learn to make a point without impaling anyone on it.

*Dear God, help us to hold all of our words
up to the light of your Son's words:
"Love one another as I have loved you."
Please forgive us when we fail to do so
and our words hurt others. Amen.*

Exaggerations

Entertainer Robert Orben once said, "Sometimes I get the feeling the whole world is against me, but deep down I know that's not true. Some of the smaller countries are neutral."

We might do well to realize the same is true for many of our exaggerated statements. Nobody loves me. Everybody hates me. You are never on time. You always interrupt me. The whole world is against me. It's just not true. Statements that begin with "everybody," "nobody," "always," and "never" are usually acts of self-pity more than descriptions of reality.

So let's find a better way to express ourselves. Let us learn to speak the truth in love. Let us narrow our observations to "the facts, Ma'am, just the facts." Let us be freed from our grandiosity long enough to realize that most of the world could care less about the things that bother us. With such humility and honesty, we might find a better way to deal with our difficulties and disappointments. Yes, we do have problems. But most of them are not of universal concern.

May we learn to manage our exaggerations,
O God, so that we speak the truth in love.
May we view life's difficulties with honesty and great hope
because we are your children. Amen.

Buttons

Somebody said people are a lot like buttons—they tend to pop off at the wrong time. Have you found that to be true? People who lose buttons in public places are usually embarrassed. People who pop off at the wrong time have to deal with embarrassment too. So if you are prone to speak before you think, give advice when none is needed, or find yourself determined to offer an opinion, consider these tried-and-true criteria for speaking.

Is it true? Within yourself, give an honest answer. Gossip spreads like wildfire and does a lot of damage. You can choose to never let gossip come from your lips.

Is it necessary? Many truths are not ours to tell. Just because it is factual does not mean it is fruitful. Some things just do not merit repeating.

Is it kind? Will it build another up to tear another down? Is it criticism with a purpose or anger out of hand?

*If the tale we are about to tell passes this test,
then we can tell it without fear of embarrassment.
Help us to think before we speak, dear Lord.
Let our words encourage one another. Amen.*

 # Community

Serving Others

When it comes to serving others, have you included those in the close quarters of your own family? We are placed in the world not to be served but to serve. Service is an admirable quality to acquire and practice, but I have noticed over the years that it is easier to serve those far away than those nearby. A businessman may drive three hours in the pouring rain to help a client and then complain mightily that his wife wants him to pick up some milk from the grocery on the way home. A teenager may travel to Mexico to repair houses and help the needy but resist the simplest of chores around the house. A homemaker may joyfully prepare her favorite dish for a community function but privately resent the daily routine of feeding her family.

Maybe it's time we brought our spirit of service home. When people work together, pull together, and serve together, a spirit of community develops that is powerful and transforming. Deep feelings of affection flow. And people feel needed and useful. Try it! You may like it!

Dear God, Jesus taught us to serve others, using the example of washing the feet of his disciples. Help us to remember that our family members are among those we are called to serve. May our family members recognize Jesus in our actions at home. Amen.

Blackballed

Jessica was a tall, slender, sixteen-year-old member of an active church youth group. One night Jessica got a call notifying her she had been blackballed by the sorority she wanted to join. The trauma of rejection was too much for Jessica—she passed out, had to be hospitalized, and refused to be comforted. Then one day, twenty members of her youth group came for a visit. Ronnie, one of the group's leaders, stepped forward and said, "God don't never blackball nobody, and neither do we." In that community of young believers, Jessica found comfort and the courage she needed to carry on.

How are you fixed for friends? Do you have a community of people who are in your corner when the blows are harsh? We were not created to face our troubles alone. We are made for community. While communities can be selective, rejecting, and extremely hurtful, other groups are welcoming, supportive, caring, and give us great feelings of belonging. I hope you have people who pick you up when the world slaps you down.

*Loving God, help us to work to make
any communities we're part of
to be welcoming, supporting, and caring.
Give us the courage to remove ourselves from
communities that are not. Amen.*

Rebuilding

I watched two children on a beach one summer day, a boy and a girl playing in the sand. They worked hard building an elaborate sand castle by the water's edge, with gates and towers and moats and inner passages. Just when they had nearly finished their project, a big wave came along and knocked it down, reducing their creation to a heap of wet sand. I expected the children to burst into tears, devastated by the destruction of their castle. Instead, they ran up the shore, laughing and holding hands and then sat down to build another castle.

Somewhere along the shores of our lives, a wave will come by and knock down what we have worked so hard to build up. We have no control over the tides of time. But if, in our building, we have also developed enduring relationships, we will be able to take each others' hands, move up the beach, and begin to build again.

When the waves of life knock down dreams,
may we be part of others' rebuilding,
and may they be part of ours, dear God.
We know that you will be within
the knocking down and the rebuilding. Amen.

Completing or Competing?

Completing one another is more important than competing with one another. Did you get that? Let me say it again. Completing one another is more important than competing with one another. In our dog-eat-dog, winner-take-all kind of world, maybe we need to ponder this alternative principle of life. Oscar Wilde once said, "Anybody can sympathize with the sufferings of a friend, but it requires a very fine nature to sympathize with a friend's success." Do you rejoice with those who rejoice as well as you weep with those who weep?

TV reality shows remind us that people will jump from fast moving vehicles, eat all kinds of worms, and perform dangerous stunts to beat others in a feverish game of competition. I wonder how far most of us would be willing to go in a friendly game of cooperation?

Maybe it's time to value interdependence over independence. Ask not "what's in this for me?" Ask "what good will this do for us all?"

Loving God, open our hearts that we may rejoice with those who rejoice and weep with those who weep. May we complete one another rather than compete with one another.

Missing Link

In Wendell Berry's novel *Jayber Crowe*, Jayber's parents died young, and the relatives that took Jayber in also died while Jayber was just a child. That got Jayber sent to the Good Shepherd Orphanage, where his needs were met, but his soul was lonely. There the staff tried to make a good Christian out of Jayber, but never offered him a sense of belonging. After Jayber left the orphanage, he wandered a while, flunked out of college, acted out some of his hurt, and finally, at the age of twenty-two, returned to the tiny town of Port William, the place of his birth. There Jayber became the community barber. By joining himself to others in both their joys and pains, Jayber, through the years, found the community, the love, and the belonging that he longed for.

The longer I live, the more I am convinced that the missing link in most of our lives is community. Loneliness is no respecter of age, affluence, class, or creed. It attacks us all. So if you, like Jayber, have a missing link in your life, you might ease the pain by a return to community— a neighborhood, a church, some place where you belong.

*Dear Jesus, our Savior, your first churches were
small communities of believers. May we live
in community with each other.
Help us to be welcoming to those who are lonely,
that they may find joy and meaning in their lives. Amen.*

Wild Geese

Have you ever watched wild geese flying through the sky in their perfectly patterned formation? You have to wonder what keeps these birds of a feather flocking together. Not a single one flies off to do its own thing. In reality, their reliance on each other is a strictly practical matter. The goose up front faces the wind head on, causing the wind to break in power and swirl more softly around the other geese. Birds who fly behind the leader find a lesser tide of air, enabling them to last longer, journey faster, and complete the trip with energy to spare.

Here's something else about geese we need to know. No goose stays in front all the time. Leadership is shared. And all that honking you hear? It's not for earthlings to enjoy. Honking is encouragement for the lead bird to hang in there. If one goose wears out or becomes ill and falls to the ground, two other geese go to the aid of the wounded one.

I think we humans could learn a few things from these birds of the air. Geese have learned how to work together for the common good and take care of their own. Oh, that we would do the same.

*We must ask ourselves, O God, if we have strayed
from working together for the common good.
Help us to be honest in our assessment,
that in the end we will become
more faithful to your will. Amen.*

Teamwork

The key component of a great baseball team is teamwork. Teamwork consists of each person doing his or her job for the good of the whole. Imagine a baseball team whose pitcher declares, "I have no need of a shortstop." What if the left fielder protests against being replaced by a pinch hitter? Bat boys do not take the mound in critical ballgames. It takes a team to win championships. People can do together what they can never accomplish apart.

Such is the case in the big game of life. We have been taught rugged individualism. We assume we must do it all ourselves. Our goal is often to need no one, depend on no one, receive from no one. "Please, Mom, I would rather do it myself."

This philosophy of life leads to isolation and limitations. Extreme individualists make no time for community. Personal grandiosity perpetuates the myth that we must do it ourselves if we want it done right. That is simply not the truth.

*Dear God, you created us to live in community,
especially the church community.
May we let the church form us
to be good team members who are faithful to you
as we work in the other communities in our lives. Amen.*

Networking

A study out of Duke University reveals that Americans have a third fewer friends and confidants than they did just two decades go. This could be another sign that people may be living lonelier, more isolated lives. In 1985, the average American had three people in whom to confide matters that were important to them. In 2004, that number had dropped to two. One in four people have no close confidants at all.

Close relationships form a safety net. Whether it's picking up a child from day care or finding someone to help you out of the city in a hurricane, we need a few people we can depend on. Is our self-sufficient, technology-saturated world leading us to isolation and loneliness? It appears so.

So how can we develop networks of friendship and support? We can get to know our neighbors. We can join a church. We can participate in school with our children. We can invite friends over for dinner. We can take the time and make the effort to know the people around us. Sooner or later all of us will need someone to lean on. Wise are those who build their network before need arrives.

Dear Jesus, you have called us friend.
Help us to open ourselves to opportunities
to become friends with others,
even during times when doing so may be difficult. Amen.

Neighborly Deed

A woman newly motivated to reach out to her neighborhood noticed a moving van at a house nearby. The "wannabe" good neighbor went home, made a pie, and took it to the resident with the moving van out front. "Welcome to our neighborhood," said the lady to the resident who answered the door. A stunned resident replied, "I'm not coming, I'm going." When the neighbor regained her composure, she replied, "Well, keep the pie anyway as a token of something I should have done a long time ago."

When it comes to hospitality to those nearby, I suspect a lot of us could get caught in that neighbor's predicament. Most of us inhabit enormous houses where family members seldom see each other, much less their neighbors. Communities have increasingly become virtual ones where we are known not as we are but as we choose to present ourselves. We drive big SUVs, hidden behind tinted windows with onboard telephones and televisions.

Sometimes I wonder what it will take for us to come out of our hiding and become a community again.

Dear Lord, open our awareness of those around us so that we can be good neighbors both when it's time to welcome and when it's time to bid farewell. Amen.

Friends

Two friends were traveling in the woods when they encountered a bear. The younger man climbed a tree and huddled between the branches. The older man, too feeble to climb, fell on the ground and played dead. The bear sniffed around him from head to toe and finally left. Together again on the trail, the young man asked the old man, "Did the bear say anything when he was sniffing your ear?"

"Sure did," replied the old man. "He said never travel again with a friend who deserts you at the first sign of danger."

Friends are the people who come in when everyone else is going out. They stick around when the going is difficult and the road is treacherous. Friends do not have all the answers, but they do stay for the conversation. They listen more than they speak. They assure more than they advise. Their presence is more comforting than a hundred books on consolation.

How are you fixed for friends? Most people have a lot of acquaintances but few friends. And that's all right. It is enough to have a person or two who are not afraid of bears.

*Dear Friend Jesus, help us to be friends
who stay through thick and thin,
who listen as well as speak, who speak the truth in love,
who accept rather than reject. Amen.*

Loneliness

Why am I so lonely? Do you ever ask that question? An entry on a website called *Lonely Life* includes these comments from a lady named Amanda: "I'm living in New York City. I miss my family really bad. My boyfriend dumped me. I lost my job. I'm feeling very, very lonely tonight—lonely enough to Google loneliness."

Loneliness may be reaching epidemic proportions in America. In 1985, ten percent of Americans said they had no close friends. By 2004, that number had risen to 24.6 percent of Americans. Are you one of the lonely?

There are some things we can do to combat loneliness. We can cultivate a friendship with the Divine. There are holes in our souls and hurts in our hearts that only God can heal. And we can connect with communities of people who know how to care and treat us fairly. Healthy communities respect people. They express compassion without encouraging enmeshment. Everybody needs somebody to lean on.

*Dear God, help us to find healthy communities
where we can feel your presence,
witness your compassion at work, and find good friends.
The help us to be good members of that community. Amen.*

December

Remember When

Do you remember when sugarplums danced in your head, when the silent night was an exciting night, when away in the manger didn't seem so far away? Why not begin this Christmas by reclaiming the child within?

So many things separate us from the true meaning of Christmas. We have food to cook and presents to open. There are trips to make and family to entertain. It's hard even at Christmas to walk upon the midnight clear and hear the angels sing.

So why not give yourself a present this holiday? Before the hustle and bustle of the day, create a quiet space in your heart. Listen to the angels sing about peace on earth, good will to all. Remember that you decide if your day is chaotic or calm, crazy or peaceful.

Once upon a time, you were able to approach Christmas with glee. Dreams danced in your head, and hope filled the air. Why not let the Child of Christmas lead you to that childlike time again?

O Child of Christmas, help us to reconnect
with the child deep within so that with great joy
we may receive you as the greatest gift of all. Amen.

Just One Candle

The Christmas song "One Little Candle" sings: "If everyone lit just one little candle, what a bright world this would be." I think about that statement every time I see a sanctuary overflowing with lighted candles on Christmas Eve. Faith is stronger than fear. Hope is greater than despair. Light is shining in the darkness, and the darkness cannot put it out.

Maybe now more than ever before, we need to let the light of love, hope, and peace shine. Let it shine in our homes and offices. Let it shine in our communities and cities. Let the whole world know that the dark acts of terrorism will never stand the test of time.

So this Christmas, light a candle of hope. Join thousands of others who are determined to brighten the corner where they are.

*Dear God of the Old Testament and the New,
you said through your prophet Isaiah that those who have
walked in darkness have seen a great light.
May we walk in the light of Christ
and be a light in your world. Amen.*

Christmas Message

According to a *Newsweek* magazine poll, eight percent off Americans believe God created the universe. In spite of our political posturing and atheistic attacks on the existence of God, there remains in the human heart a belief in the sacred. Or, as George Weigel says, "We are not congealed stardust, an accidental by-product of some cosmic chemistry. We are not just something, we are someone."

As persons of value, created in the image of our Maker, it behooves us to become all we are created to be. The Christian message of Christmas, often hidden in the commercialism of the season, is that God not only made us, but God came in the person of Jesus Christ to show us the way to live. Love, joy, peace, hope—those words we so casually toss around this time of year—are more than utopian ideas. They are the core values of human life as it was intended to be.

So never settle for being something when you are capable of becoming someone. Never let the world squeeze you into the mold of being a customer, a number, an occupation, or one more humanoid on the planet earth. You are a child of God.

Creator God, help us to take the words we hear at Christmas
—love, joy, peace, and hope—
and make them values we live by throughout the year.
May we remember that we are your children. Amen.

God Comes to Earth

Pope John XXIII brought many reforms to the Catholic Church. He also made great efforts to connect with people. On the day after Christmas one year, Pope John decided to visit one of the worst prisons in Rome. It was the first time in ninety years that a pope had gone to a prison. On that historic occasion, this is what he said to the inmates: "You could not come to me, so I have come to you!"

From a Christian point of view, that is what Christmas is all about. Christmas is more than buttons and bows, toys and clothes, family dinners and fellowship gatherings. Christmas is the Christian affirmation that God broke into human history in the form of a child. Christians and non-Christians alike ask, "What child is this?" And Christians reply, "This is Christ the King, whom shepherds guard and angels sing." Christmas for Christians is the glad and glorious announcement that God decided to come to us when we found it impossible to connect with him.

So without hesitation, let Christians join the glad celebration. And let us be respectful of those who do not share our beliefs.

*O God of the angels' song, you loved us
so much that you came to earth in the form of a child
born in a manger. This Christmas, let the
good news of Jesus' birth open our eyes. Amen.*

Not Too Late

One of the hundreds of takeoffs on *The Night before Christmas* goes like this: "'Twas the night before Jesus, when all through the earth, every creature was stirring for a Savior's new birth. Christ was on earth, old things were like new. People were seeing what God can do."

On this eve of Christ's birth, you can have a new beginning. The old can be forgiven, the new can be enlivened. Love, joy, and peace can take root way down in the depths of your heart. There is still time to start over. There is still grace to see you through. There is still hope to lift you up. There is still life to be lived. It may be too late to shop. It is not too late to start a new life.

If you could use a little Good News tonight, if just once you'd like to hear about lifting people up instead of putting people down, find a faith community and rejoice with them this December.

Loving God, each Christmas an invitation from you to experience love, joy, and peace comes into our hearts. May we gladly accept your invitation to enjoy a new beginning. Amen.

Silence

How silently, how silently, the first gift of Christmas was given. While bars bustled in Bethlehem and visitors scrambled to find a place to sleep, Christ our Savior was born. Just the thought of the true meaning of Christmas blows our minds. If God is willing to enter a manger, is there any place on earth that God is not willing to go?

In all our efforts at political correctness, social acceptance, and just plain inattentiveness, I wonder if we, too, miss the true meaning of Christmas. Yes, Christmas is a religious holiday. Yes, Christmas is distinctly Christian. Certainly people of other faiths ought not to feel compelled to observe this holy day that has become a cultural holiday. Beyond the hype, the hustle, the harried customs of the season, there lies a deep theological truth. Christ our Savior is born. May Christians be sensitive enough to stop and ponder their beliefs without being offensive to people of other faiths.

Dear God, this Christmas, may we ask ourselves
where we are willing to go with you.
Give us courage and vision to venture
beyond what is familiar in your name. Amen.

Good News

It was a large, impressive waiting room filled with the finest furniture and stocked with the latest information. On this particular day, the place was packed with people waiting to see one of several physicians. An elderly lady sat in one corner of that waiting room, crying. At first, she wept quietly. But as the hopes and fears of all her years mounted in her mind, she began to sob openly.

There was, in that waiting room, a toddler, playing with toys carefully chosen from his mother's purse. Seeing the woman in tears, the kid climbed down from his chair, toddled over to her and, touching the lady on the cheek, said, "It's all right, it's all right, everything is going to be all right." The woman smiled.

The good news of Christmas is that the Christ child has entered our frightening world. Climbing down from his throne in glory and touching with his kindness, he says, "It's all right, it's all right; even when everything seems wrong, it will be all right." May the whole world feel that touch and be able to smile.

*Help us, O God of Christmas, to share your good news with
all of our neighbors—here and around the world—that your Son
has come, and everything will be all right.
Thank you for such good news. Amen.*

Little Things

We do everything in big ways these days. Have you noticed that? We have big malls, big churches, big sales, big stars, and big events. Everything we do this year must be bigger and better than last year. Ah, that is the American way.

In our fascination with big things, are we missing the meaning of small things? Mother Theresa once said, "We cannot do great things on this earth. We can only do little things with great love." Some people think they would be generous if only they could win the lottery. Others see great reason to serve—if the cameras are rolling for the big story on the evening news.

Meanwhile, we celebrate Christmas—the birth of a helpless baby more powerful than Herod's armies. In a stable, not a stateroom, the course of history was changed.

Little things done in loving ways still have power to change the world. A hug, a handshake, a touch of kindness, a gift of love—all have eternal dimensions that we never dream of. So this Christmas, whatever good we can do, life we can share, love we can spread, let us neither defer it nor neglect it. Let us do it now.

Loving God, this Christmas may we not hesitate to express seemingly small acts of love and kindness, for we know that in your eyes those are the great acts you call us to do. Amen.

Christmas Tree

It all happened one December in the suburb of a city. A few weeks before Christmas, a tree was dropped in the center of a cul-de-sac. How it got there nobody knows. Somebody, however, put it in a stand. Somebody else wrapped it in tinsel. Each day the number of ornaments grew. Then, on Christmas Eve, a creche was added, too. There in the center of asphalt bare, stood a beautiful symbol of neighbors who share.

The Christmas Spirit calls people everywhere from isolation into community, from self-centeredness into service, from loneliness into loveliness. When people work together, lives, even more so than trees, take shape and become beautiful. We can make a difference. We can develop cities with liberty and justice for all. We can clean up the environment. We can ensure equal opportunity. We can do something significant with our lives.

So how about it? Are you doing something this December to make your neighborhood a special, beautiful place to remind people that love came down at Christmas?

O Lord, Giver of the Greatest Gift,
may we live the spirit of Christmas this holy season.
Help us to be good news to those around us,
to take shape and make lives beautiful. Amen.

Too Good to Be True

In the classic Christmas movie, *Miracle on 34th Street*, Santa Claus is put on trial in New York City for spreading cheer and good will among people. His principles of consideration and cooperation prove to be threatening in a world of competition.

I suppose the message of Christmas always seems too good to be true, too miraculous to be mixed into everyday life. After all, we are practical people pounding out a living in a pragmatic kind of world. We take what we want and earn what we need and try to get ahead without falling too far behind.

In our efforts to make a living, have we missed the meaning of life? Where is the joy? How about peace that passes the understanding of present circumstances? Could you use some of that for Christmas? Is hope alive and well in the depths of your soul? Will you have enough love to go around for the holidays?

We may debate the existence of the white-bearded man in the red suit, but the things he stands for we cannot live without.

O God, may we take the angel song of peace and good will to heart. Let us bring the joy, hope, and love of the Christmas message to someone who needs to experience it anew. Amen.

Wants

"What do you want for Christmas?" That's a constant question asked in December. Ask any child on the street what they want for Christmas, and you will get a quick and descriptive reply.

Through the years, I've made another observation about our wants and wishes for Christmas. Sometimes we get what we want and wind up not wanting what we get. A woman won millions of dollars in a state lottery. She quit her job, bought a new house, purchased the car of her dreams, and made wise investments that enabled her to live comfortably on the interest. A dream had come true. She had it made.

But not really. Pretty soon she was bored silly. She became suspicious of her new-found friends and longed for the good times with her old neighbors. She missed the challenge of her old job. She constantly worried about her investments. A dream became a nightmare. She got what she wanted, but wound up not wanting what she got.

What do you want for Christmas?

This Christmas, dear God, let us examine our wants
to know whether they reflect your kingdom values
or the values of a society that values power and things.
May we grow in our generosity,
that we will work for your kingdom on earth. Amen.

Church Attendance

According to researcher George Barna, forty percent of Americans say their favorite weekly activity is attending church. Maybe those boring sermons and stiff necked music are not as disengaging as you once thought them to be! Evidently a lot of people find something meaningful, something powerful, something worthwhile in church. Church is a meeting place with God. While it is possible to run into God almost anywhere in the world, people who are looking for God rightfully try to find God at God's house.

There are people at church, all kinds of people—people we like, people we wonder about, "normal" people, "odd" people. They are sort of like the people you may meet at any community event—except for one thing. People at church are committed to community; they have the desire to become the visible body of Christ on earth. They gather in a spirit of service instead of a spirit of selfishness.

So if it's been awhile since you've attended a church service, if you are sensing that something might be missing in your life, Advent, the four weeks before Christmas when we prepare for Christ's birth anew, is a good time to talk with God and to be with God's people.

Dear God, your Son said that he is wherever two or three are gathered in his name. May we be part of a community of people who love you and want to be the visible body of Christ on earth. Amen.

Easter People

The Gambler

Famous British World War I Royal Air Force Pilot Studdert Kennedy wrote:

> "He was a gambler, too, my Christ.
> He took His life and threw
> It for a world redeemed.
> And ere His agony was done,
> Before the weltering sun went down,
> Crowning that day with its crimson crown,
> He knew that He had won."

In the midst of all the confusing stories of Good Friday and the mysterious appearances of Easter Sunday, there lies a profound truth that has changed the world. God so loved us humans that he gave his son Jesus to restore us to life. That message of hope has shaped culture and transformed lives for centuries. In the struggle between good and evil, good wins. In the strife between truth and falsehood, truth triumphs. In our fierce battle to find our purpose for living, God comes on a rescue mission to save us.

Are you living on the Easter side of life?

Thank you, O God, for loving us so much that
you gave us your Son to show us how to live
and to teach about your grace and forgiveness.
May we live on the Easter side. Amen.

Miracle Road

Randal McCloy went home from the hospital a few weeks ago. He was the sole survivor of a mining accident last January in Morgantown, West Virginia. Randall was greeted by family and friends, who renamed the rural road on which Randal lives. That road is now named "Miracle Road" in honor of Randal McCloy. Randal's physician, Dr. Russell Biundo, told reporters this was like a resurrection for Randal. He's a new person, a different person, a person with a whole new life ahead of him.

I suppose most of us could benefit from a resurrection like that. There are times when we need to take our old lives, stained and blotted, and trade them for new ones, all unspotted. We need a new beginning, a transformation, yes, even a personal resurrection.

All of that is possible through faith in the resurrection of Jesus Christ. Easter is more than a holiday. Easter is a new way of seeing, believing, acting, living. It's a brand new life for people like you and me.

Dear God of Easter morning, this Easter
help us to see things with new eyes
and embrace the new life you offer us.
May we accept the brand new life you offer. Amen.

Glad Affirmation

The early Greek Orthodox Church had an unusual custom. The week after Easter, clergy and laity would gather in the sanctuary to tell jokes, stories, and anecdotes. It was not a comedy night, but a celebration day. It was a glad and happy way for people to resonate with the big joke God pulled on Satan by raising Jesus from the dead. It was the glad affirmation that life is stronger than death, forgiveness trumps guilt, and we are all winners in the eternal scheme of things. I kind of like that custom. How about you?

Easter is more than one big day at church. Easter is a way of life, a way of seeing, an attitude of being that permeates our daily routines and orders each step we take. We have good reason to face every trouble with the glad assurance that "this too will pass." We have the bold faith to look death in the eye and know this is not the final word, for life is stronger than death. We have the comfort to know that weeping may last for a night, but joy comes in the morning. So, let the jokes start. Let the laughter begin. Let hope reign!

*O God of Easter, let the joy and hope of Easter Sunday
permeate our lives throughout the year.
Help us to remember that the hope Easter brings
reigns through good times and bad. Amen.*

Trouble Happens

Trouble happens. Have you come to accept that? Never morning wears to evening but some heart breaks, a heart just as sensitive as yours and mine. That's life. So through the week that Christians call Holy Week, we walk the Via Delarosa—the trail of tears, the road of sorrow, the path of crucifixion. We revisit the scenes of kangaroo courts, screaming crowds, scheming priests, and secular politicians who prefer to wash their hands of the whole thing. Why do Christians do this? Do we enjoy brutality? Hardly! We are simply realists who are willing to admit that trouble comes to one and all.

We also relive this tale of trouble in the sure and certain hope that no problem enjoys everlasting life. Every sunset brings with it the sure and certain hope of a sunrise. This, too, is life. We are Resurrection people, and come Sunday, we will shout from the rooftops that "Christ the Lord is Risen!"

We are Resurrection people, O God,
and so we shout, "Christ the Lord is risen!"
today, tomorrow, and all of our days.
So be it! Amen.

The Bumblebee

According to extensive aeronautical research, it is impossible for the bumblebee to fly. It's built all wrong, with proportions in inappropriate places. According to aeronautical designs, the bumblebee had better get used to walking. Of course, no one has been able to communicate that to the bumblebee. So it just keeps on spreading its wings, flying from one flower to another, even though from a human perspective, it's impossible.

People are most productive when they attempt the impossible, too. To dream impossible dreams, to fight unbeatable foes, to overcome unbelievable odds and, yes, to reach for the stars—that is our quest. That is our purpose. That is our goal. Easter is the glad celebration of life against all odds. It is hope beyond all defeat. It is courage to face all foes.

*Dear God of bumblebees and all other
marvels of creation, may we, like the bumblebee,
not limit ourselves only to what seems possible to us.
You are a big God. May we do great things
for you and in your name. Amen.*

Sacrificial Love

At the young age of twenty-five, our son underwent open-heart surgery to replace a defective valve. He was scared; I was concerned. As I leaned over the hospital bed to hug him on the morning of his surgery, I said, "I wish I could take your place today and endure this surgery for you." With a tear in his eye, Wes responded, "I wish you could too."

As we enter a week that Christians call holy, that is exactly what happened centuries ago. God in the person of Jesus Christ took our place on the cross of Calvary. Parents understand love like that. Who of us would not gladly bear the pain of our children if we could? As a father loves his children, so God loves us. When it came time to bear the sin that causes us dis-ease, Christ took our place.

So Christians around the world this week gather in elaborate cathedrals and simple sanctuaries to say, "Thank you." Thank You, Jesus, for saving my soul. Thank you, Jesus, for making me whole!

Dear God, only you know how each of us needs to be made whole. Open us to the Holy Spirit's work within us that we may travel our journey toward wholeness. Thank you for the hope that Easter brings. Amen.

Faith, Hope, & Love

It's Not Fair!

In a *Peanuts* cartoon, Lucy and Charlie Brown are walking home from school. Lucy has a report card in her hand and is clearly unhappy. She turns to Charlie Brown and complains, "It's just not fair, Charlie Brown. It's just not fair. I studied a whole week for my math exam. Sally only studied two hours. She got an A. I got a C. Life is just not fair."

I hear that lament quite often. How about you? Some folks work all their lives and barely make a living. Somebody else buys one ticket and wins the lottery. Some people live a healthy life, exercise regularly, watch what they eat, but still wind up with cancer. Others smoke, drink, abuse their bodies, and still manage to live a long time. Life is not always fair.

When things fail to turn out the way they should and you wind up on the short end of the stick, what do you do? Get bitter? Get depressed? Turn sour on life? Or do you find a faith to carry on, a courage to keep believing, a hope that we will understand it better by and by?

Compassionate God, strengthen our faith so that when times become difficult—and they will—we can trust that you will be with us and will see us through. Equip us with a faith to carry on. Amen.

From Fear to Faith

In Robert Hicks's stirring novel *Widow of the South*, Carrie McGavock tries to make sense out of the death of her own children, not to mention the dying soldiers being brought to her plantation from the bloody Civil War Battle of Franklin. As Carrie weighs her thoughts, she comes to this conclusion: "My children had not been taken, they had just died. Just died, no special significance to it, no betrayal. He had not been there, there had been no purpose to their deaths, no purpose to the intervening years of my morning. I passed from fear to love in that instant."

"Everything happens for a reason." That is a saying woven deep into the religious culture of our day. So people are constantly trying to discover the reason behind some accident, some illness, some misfortune that has come their way. What if Carrie is right? What if some things do not happen for a reason? What if some things just happen? What if there is neither rhyme nor reason to some riddles of life? Such thoughts may leave more questions than they answer, but they may also free us to move from fear to faith.

No matter what happens, O Lord,
you are Emanuel, "God with us."
Help us to increase our faith and so not live in fear.
May we move from fear to faith. Amen.

Into Deep Waters

A speedboat driver hit a wave at high speed that propelled him out of the boat and deep into the water. The driver explained his experience this way: "I was so deep that I lost my sense of direction. I had no idea which way was up. Fortunately, I remained calm and let the buoyancy of the lifejacket do its job. As it began pulling me toward the surface, I could then swim for help."

I run into a lot of people who have been thrown into the deep waters of life. We experience a job loss, a divorce, a life-threatening illness, or an untimely death of a loved one. The shock of such deep waters causes us to lose our sense of direction. In times like these, we can easily make things worse by trying too hard to take matters into our own hands. When we feel out of control, it is natural to try to get control of something or someone. We will be wise to resist that temptation. Trying to make things better, we can easily make things worse. Such times call for faith and trust. Let the buoyancy of life, the grace of God, and the goodness of friends restore your sense of direction.

O God, out of the depths we cry to you.
May we put our faith and trust in you,
that you will guide us through our most difficult times.
Let us hold to the hope that Jesus brought to us
when he walked among us. Amen.

Letting Go

A little boy asked his grandmother how old she was. The grandmother, not interested in revealing her age, replied, "I'm 39 and holding."

The little boy, sensing he had not received a straight answer, continued, "And, Grandmother, how old would you be if you let go?"

Holding on seems to be a common problem of life. We work hard to hold on to our youth, denying the physical evidence of our years. We hold on to relationships that have long since passed us by. We hold on to the past even though we know it will not change the future. We like to hold on. There seems to be some security in "what was," even though such security is an illusion.

So maybe it's time to own our fears of letting go. A father described to me the pain he felt when bringing his child to day school the first time. A mother cries even more tears as she tells me the pain of taking her last child to college. I have held the hand of many people trying to let go of a loved one at death. No, no, it's never easy to let go. Yet the goal of life is to die with open hands, not clinched fists.

Loving God, help us know when it is time to let go.
May we do so, knowing that you hold all things in your hands.
In the name of Jesus, who, after a struggle,
knew when it was time to let go. Amen.

Stars Shining Bright

Helen Keller once said, "I will love the light for it shows me the way, yet I will endure the darkness for it shows me the stars." Let's read that again: "I will love the light for it shows me the way, yet I will endure the darkness for it shows me the stars."

So the old principle is true. The stars shine brightest on the darkest of nights. I enjoy the sunlight. The sun lifts our spirits and brightens our days. The sun shines with opportunity and possibility. The sun calls us to activity and action.

But what about the night? The night can be fearful. It can be long. The night can be troubling. It often brings out the wrong. We avoid the dark by trying to give it light.

But there is something else about the night that we need to know. The stars shine at night. The darker the night, the brighter the stars. The stars give us direction. The stars give us hope. The stars cause us to look to the heavens from whence our help comes. So, fear not your night. The stars are shining bright.

*O God of glad tidings, you sent a star
to point the way for the wise men.
May we remember that great star when our nights
seem the darkest. Help us to be hopeful people. Amen.*

Our Song

Poet Emily Dickinson wrote:

> "Hope is the thing with feathers
> That perches in the soul,
> And sings the tune without the words,
> And never stops at all."

As I listen to the birds whistle their spring tunes each morning, I am amazed at the determination of birds to keep singing. Oh, I know. We sometimes long to be as free as a bird. From the inside looking out, birds appear to have it made—no alarm clocks, no appointments, no meetings to attend or dates to keep. But is the life of a bird all that great? They are exposed to all kinds of weather while I relax securely in the comfort of my home. They are constantly rebuilding their houses while I have to only maintain my own. Yes, life is often miserable for a bird, yet birds keep on singing.

What has life done to your song? Is there still a tune in your heart that never stops at all? Birds sing because birds have wings. If the branch breaks, the bird flies. So can you and I. Since most things worth doing aren't completed in this lifetime, let us keep hope alive.

Loving God, may we keep a song in our hearts
even if all seems not to be going well.
We place our trust in you, knowing that
you hold the future in your hands. Amen.

Filled with Joy

Bethany Hamilton, once ranked as the best amateur teen surfer in Hawaii, lost an arm to a tiger shark in 2003. The injury, however, has not destroyed Bethany's compassion and competitiveness. She is back surfing, competing with the best athletes, determined to move on to the next level. In a recent TV interview, Bethany said, "I'm looking forward to the future. I want to show the world that I still have a life, and that my life is filled with joy."

Is your life filled with that kind of joy? In one way or another, all of us live handicapped lives. We don't have the brightest brain in the company. We don't have the greatest skill on the team. Hurts and heartaches of the past come back to haunt us in the night. We did not get a great start, and we are uncertain about our finish.

So what can we do? We can face each handicap with courage. We can keep a positive attitude. We can do what we can with what we've got. We can rejoice and be glad each day. We can show the world that we still have a life.

O Lord, in spite of disabilities and heartaches,
we rejoice this day and are glad in it.
Give us courage that makes us glad
and help us to stay positive. Amen.

The World in His Hands

I love to visit New York City. Down on Fifth Avenue in front of the RCA building, there is a statue of Atlas struggling and straining trying to hold the world on his shoulders. Across the street behind the high altar in St. Patrick's Cathedral is a statue of the boy Jesus, eight or nine years old, holding the whole world in one hand with no effort at all.

When I am troubled, filled with pain, anxious about my future and uncertain about my gain, I am comforted to know that God has the whole world in his hands. He is not struggling over my destiny. He is neither overwhelmed by my neediness nor confused about my concerns. He who made the stars to shine at night holds my destiny in his hands. I cannot drift beyond God's love and care.

Have you discovered that kind of God? The God we need to know is not just way out there in the distant regions of the universe. He is down here in the nitty-gritty of our day-to-day lives, helping us make sense out of the most senseless days and the most troubling circumstances.

O God, you are here among us
and for that we are very grateful.
May we open our eyes to your presence
and draw strength and hope from it. Amen.

Darkness

Author Marilyn McEntrye offers this advice on how to make it through the dark places of our lives: "Go slowly. Consent to it, but don't wallow in it. Know the darkness can be a place of germination and growth. Take an outstretched hand if you find one. Remember the light. Watch for the dawn."

Our days will not be fair always. Into every life there comes a dark night of the soul and periods of struggle where the way is not clear and helpful directions seem distant. In times like these, we need to hang on, endure, anticipate the dawn. Darkness calls for caution. We can be circumspect without being crushed. We can be helped without being hurt. Even in the darkness, we can live by hope.

A very wise psalmist said a long time ago, "Weeping may last for the night, but joy comes in the morning." Even when the nights are long, the day breaks and the sun rises. The morning light overcomes the evening shadows. We can see again. We can walk again. We can have confidence again. So the next time you are trying to find your way through the dark, remember the dark moments never last forever.

*"By your tender mercy, O God,
the dawn from on high will break upon us
to give light to those who sit in darkness and in the shadow of death,
to guide our feet into the way of peace."* Amen.

Droughts of the Soul

Last summer, the Southeastern United States suffered the worst drought in more than a hundred years. It got so severe that the city of Atlanta came within ninety days of running out of water. The tiny town of Orme, Tennessee, was hauling water from northern Alabama and limiting water usage to three hours a day. Singer Michael W. Smith and the Mayor of Atlanta were calling on people to pray for rain. Last summer was dry; it was really dry.

Droughts invade the soul as well as the soil. There are spiritual deserts that must be navigated in the pursuit of a fruitful life. What does one do when your soul lands in the dry winds of the desert? Let me suggest a thing or two. Stick together. People in grief and guilt often isolate themselves from the very source of their healing. We create our own droughts because we separate ourselves from the people who can help us. Secondly, we can keep hope alive. It always rains. There are streams that appear in the desert, and we must count on them for soul survival.

*Our souls wait for you, O Lord; for our hope lies in you.
In difficult times we pray that our souls be calmed
as we live in faith that you will bring a better time.
Thank you for being in the desert with us. Amen.*

People of Hope

A father and son planned a camping trip for just the two of them. When it was time to go to bed, the little boy was so excited that he could not sleep. Finally he trudged down the hall to his Dad's room, shook him awake and said, "I'm too excited about our trip tomorrow to go to sleep."

"I know," replied the Dad, "but you have to go back to bed and get some rest."

So the kid reluctantly headed back to his bed. Before long, he was back in his Dad's room, poking him awake again. "What do you want now?" asked the sleepy father.

"I just want to thank you for all the fun we're going to have tomorrow," said the boy.

Are you anticipating your future with that kind of excitement? Are you standing on tiptoe, awaiting tomorrow? People of hope not only claim the present but also affirm the future. They are not only grateful for what is; they are also thankful for what is going to be. When I think of God and all God has done for me, and when I think of all God has in store for me, I just want to stop and say, "Thank you, God, for tomorrow."

May we wait patiently but with great expectancy for your will to be accomplished in your earthly kingdom. In our patient, expectant waiting, help us discover and welcome what you would have us to do and to be. Amen.

Losses

A friend of mine describes the grief of losing her husband as "amputation without an anesthetic." Perhaps she is right.

Life is full of losses. We not only lose soul mates of many years, we lose jobs and friends and even parts of our body one piece at a time. All of life is an education in letting go. Death is deadly. Divorce is damaging. Job insecurity is reality.

So what can we do with such pain? We can repress it and pretend it doesn't hurt. We can succumb to it and lose our zest for life. Or we can walk through the valley and learn new lessons for life. We can discover that we are stronger than we thought we were. We can find that we have friends we never knew we had. We can discover that God never leaves us or forsakes us.

Walking through the dark shadows of sorrow, my friend made this discovery: "Not once did the birds stop singing."

Now there is a hope worth living for.

*O God of steadfast love, even in our most barren of times
you never leave us. So let us place our trust in you,
knowing that in spite of our losses you offer
a brighter tomorrow. Amen.*

What Makes the World Go 'Round?

What makes the world go 'round? Do you ever ask that question? Many would say that money makes the world go 'round. How else can one explain our obsession with the stock market? Some might say that power makes the world go 'round. That could be the reason why Nashville's mayor would spend over two million dollars to get elected to a job that pays $136,000.

Great leaders of history like John Wesley, Mahatma Gandhi, and Martin Luther King, Jr., had a better idea. They believed that love makes the world go 'round—not some warm, topsy-turvy, spine-tingling feeling talked about in popular songs, but a deep, abiding respect for all people that enables us to live together as brothers and sisters rather than perish apart as fools.

The world needs a fresh breeze of deep, loving respect blowing across our land. We can do better than demonize those who differ from others. Can we not once more learn to love our neighbors as we love ourselves?

*Dear God, you gave us two great commandments—
to love God and to love our neighbor as we love ourselves.
Forgive us for our lack of understanding when we think
we can do one without doing the other. May our love for God
and for our neighbors grow. Amen.*

Love Power

Napoleon looked back over the years of his life and said, "Alexander, Caesar, Charlemagne, and I have founded great empires; but upon what did these creations of our genius depend? Upon force. Jesus alone founded His empire upon love, and today millions will die for him." So, we are reminded once again that love is the most durable power in the world.

Force can conquer, but love alone inspires. Persuasion can excite, but only love unites. Coercion may capture people for a while, but only love goes the second mile.

So when are we going to capture the forces of love for the good of the world? There are certainly evidences of love power in the generous outpouring of relief to the people devastated by the tsunami in Southeast Asia. There are glimpses of love power when people of different minds are willing to meet at the common table of discussion instead of retiring to their respective corners to commence in shouting. Love is comfortable with small beginnings and can endure the test of time. So why not put some love power in your life?

Dear God of unconditional love, you called us to show your love to the world. We seem to have forgotten that call. Forgive us, God. Help us to work together for the common good, knowing that all of us are your children. Amen.

Elephant Man

Elephant Man, by Christine Sparks, is a marvelous story about John Merrick, who, suffering from a deforming disease and put on display at freak shows, was rescued to life by a surgeon named Frederick Treves. Treves gave Merrick a room at the hospital and started treating the strange-looking man as a human being instead of a wild animal. The transformation was amazing. Instead of being a wild beast, the elephant man turned out to be a gentle, affectionate, lovable human being without an unkind word for anyone. Treves had people visit Merrick in the hospital and slowly this man, abandoned by his mother at age four and treated like an animal all of his life, discovered his humanity. To each new life experience, Merrick responded with childlike wonder. "I am happy every hour of every day," he said.

If dignity and humanity can be restored to the elephant man, it has to be in reach of the likes of you and me. Never underestimate the power of love. Never warehouse people as worthless. Never believe people to be unredeemable.

Love can turn us around. Yes, love can make a difference.

Dear Lord, your love for us is never ending.
May we respond to your love by loving others
no matter how unlovable they may seem to us.
Let us never deem our judgment worthier than yours. Amen.

Family

Strong Children

I came upon a quote the other day, attributed to Frederick Douglass, that I think I will keep. It goes like this: "It's easier to build strong children than to repair broken adults." Let me say that again—"It's easier to build strong children than to repair broken adults."

I say hats off to parents who try their best to raise loving, responsible kids. I know it's not always easy. As one young mother of two boys, seven and nine, once lamented, "Living with these children is like trying to survive a tornado." Probably so. Yet, it's worth the effort. The world will be a better place because mothers and fathers, sometimes under very difficult circumstances, manage to form personalities and communicate values that stand the test of time.

The rest of us need to help in every way we can. Grandparents have opportunities to mentor grandchildren in ways never before imagined. The technology is available to help us learn and keep us informed in ways never even conceived a generation ago. Will we dedicate ourselves to use such advances for positive purposes?

Lord, you said to let the children come to you.
Help us to follow your example so that
we help children become strong adults, whether rearing
children ourselves or volunteering in schools or
giving our share to educate and keep them healthy. Amen.

Eating Together

"Families that eat together produce stronger, healthier, families. That's a fact," says Miriam Weinstein in her book, *The Surprising Power of Family Meals*. Families that eat together have fewer incidences of alcohol and drug abuse. Families that eat together have less obesity and fewer eating disorders. Families that eat together are more resilient and able to handle the troubles that come their way. Eating together gives children reliable access to their parents and an anchoring for everyone's day. It emphasizes belonging and community.

In the mad dash of family life, family meals often fall by the wayside. Obligations and responsibilities leave us grabbing a sandwich on the run or getting a bite to eat alone. Everyone knows that family is the foundation for a strong society. In the grand scheme of things, are we willing to do the simple things that enhance family values? Are we willing to count the cost and pay the price of carving out time for family meals for the sake of the greater good?

Dear God, help us recognize when we're not making time for things that strengthen our family life.
May we value belonging and community so that when we are away from family, we take those values with us. Amen.

Giant Faith

In Tracey Stewart's biography of her late husband, Payne, Tracey shares the ups and downs of life as a pro golfer on the PGA tour. She talks of their victories and defeats, their trials and temptations, and the foundations of their faith.

"There came a time," says Tracey, "when we wanted a stronger religious center in our home."

While she and Payne had been raised in Christian families, the pressures of travel and public appearances caused them to neglect the faith they both embraced. They especially wanted their children to be spiritually centered. So they found a church, enrolled their children in Sunday school, and began as a family to study the Bible. Then Tracey says this: "The giant faith within began to be awakened again. With new energy, Payne and I wanted to live the Christian life, not just talk about it."

Do you have that hope and dream for your family? Do you live the faith as well as talk about it? Do you make the time and set the priorities necessary for you and your children to know God?

Dear God, may we make you the center of our family life. Open all of us to helping children, those in our nuclear and extended families and those in our world community, to know your love and grace in their lives. Amen.

Inheritance

Two old gentlemen were discussing life from separate beds in a nursing home. Finally one old fella said to the other, "All my money is in a high-interest account. Every one of my relatives is highly interested in every penny of it."

Well, there's more truth in that observation than most of us want to admit. From multibillionaires to common working folk, families find multiple ways of feuding over inheritances. It continues from generation after generation, and few families are completely immune from it.

So how can families be protected from hard feelings over an inheritance? There are no guarantees, but here are a few thoughts that might help. Be smart. Plan your estate the best you can. Be open. Family secrets are the breeding ground for all kinds of hard feelings. Be fair. Never use an inheritance to get even. Be free. Do you have things, or do things have you?

And finally, remember that coveting is a top-ten sin. Teach the people you love to be lighthearted about possessions.

Help us, O God, to consider the question of whether we have things or whether things have us and then to answer it honestly. Teach us to be smart, open, fair, and free. Teach us to hold things lightly. Amen.

Conversational Opportunity

In a *Baby Blues* cartoon, parents are going in opposite directions as they rush to meet the demands of the morning. That's when the mother yells back to the father and says, "Remind me to finish the story I started to tell you this morning after the kids go to bed, but before I fall asleep or forget it all together."

Then in bold letters, readers are confronted with these words:

"The window of conversational opportunity continues to shrink."

Indeed it does!

One would think that with all the tools of modern technology, families would be communicating better than ever. Everyone is certainly talking more. But are we communicating more? Are we having meaningful conversations with significant others? It is one thing to post our thoughts and feelings on a website and quite another thing to be in touch with our families. I suspect it is always easier to be in a chat room with a stranger than to be in the dining room with relatives. What are the windows of conversational opportunity being overlooked in your house?

Dear God, may we love you enough to set aside time to talk with each other about you and your will for our families. Help us to become better listeners, both to you and to family members during those times. Amen.

Fathers

For many years, Vance rejected religious services, practiced no rituals, spurned all mainstream notions of God. He was a realist who took responsibility for himself and felt he needed no one—and certainly not the crutch of religion. After all, he had a great job, a fine education, and a family to write home about. What else could anyone want?

Then one day Vance's five-year-old daughter started asking questions about life and death. She couldn't understand why anyone would grow old and die. That's when Vance decided he could use a little help, at least with his child. So, he enrolled his daughter in a religious day school and began attending the worship services. Slowly, Vance began believing the things he never thought he needed.

There are a lot of men like Vance. Your best hope for faith is the leadership of a little child—that son or daughter whom you love so much and for whom you want only the best, the best house, the best school, the best socialization. Both of you deserve the best faith too.

Through your prophet Isaiah, O God,
you told us that a little child will lead us in your kingdom.
Help us to be like children, who accept
and love you just because. Amen.

Domestic Pain

In an episode of the TV sitcom *Roseanne*, a neighbor strolls over with a newspaper and says, "Hey, Roseanne, what do you think about this headline? 'A Utah housewife stabs her husband thirty-seven times.'"

Without hesitating, Roseanne replies, "I admire her restraint."

In the close quarters of family life, the line between comedy and tragedy is thin to say the least. Reality reminds us that a high percentage of the homicides in this country continue to take place in homes among family members. That is no laughing matter. Families fight. No one knows how to hurt us like another member of the family. Even when the pain does not erupt in violence, it gets expressed with distance, causing brothers and sisters to erase each other from their address books and e-mail files.

So how can we deal with our difficult relatives? We can be realistic rather than idealistic. We can be honest instead of pretending. We can practice restraint instead of rage. We can love our enemies even when they are related to us.

Gracious God, you have given us the gift of families and we thank you. Help us to value, love and accept each other even during the most difficult of circumstances just as you value, love, and accept us. Amen.

Lighten Up!

Did you hear about the Green Bay Packer fan who got so angry at his seven-year-old son for not wearing a team jersey that he restrained the kid in a chair for an hour and taped the jersey to him? Police arrested the thirty-six-year-old father after his wife told authorities about the incident. The father pleaded no contest to disorderly conduct and paid a fine.

That story speaks to the danger of people losing perspective in light of their passions. I like sports. They bring enjoyment to life and unity to persons who become loyal fans. But let's get real. Passion for sports is no excuse for abuse of children. Sometimes we need to lighten up.

That may be a worthwhile motto in many areas of life. Seldom is life as serious as we make it out to be. Work is important, but it is not important enough to sacrifice one's health. Families face challenges and difficulties, but some family problems simply scratch the surface instead of wounding the soul. So we must learn to be truly wise and live our lives accordingly.

O Lord, help us to discern the truly important issues that
affect our families and then to seek your will
as we work to address those issues.
Let us practice your unconditional love
within the walls of our homes. Amen.

Excellent Homes

All of us are concerned about excellent schools, excellent jobs, excellent neighborhoods, and excellent communities. Are we as equally concerned about excellent homes? And I am not referring to the price of the real estate.

Families are the foundation of society. And families are in trouble. We are simply not imparting to the next generation a set of fundamental norms and beliefs that will sustain a civilization. Our children must be capable of commitment, understand and accept responsibility, share a sense of stewardship about their communities, and be willing to work for the common good. Churches can help. Schools can do their part. Communities can provide recreational and developmental opportunities. But none can take the place of family.

Eighty-five percent of Americans believe parenting is more difficult these days than it used to be. They are probably right. But parents must not surrender to the pressures of the day. They must rise to the challenge for the sake of the world.

Help us, God, to impart healthy norms and beliefs to the next generation. Help our children to be capable of commitment, understanding, and responsibility. Amen.

Graduations

As graduation time comes and many families experience the coming and going of family members, it may be the right time to remember that children are gifts from God. They are given to us so that we can offer them a safe, loving place to grow inner and outer freedom. They are like strangers, who ask for hospitality, become good friends, and then leave again to continue their journey. A good gift is twice given—the gift we receive and the gift we give again.

It is never easy to give our children their freedom, especially in this violent and exploitative world. But they do not belong to us. They belong to God. One of the greatest acts of trust is setting our children free to explore life on their own in God's time.

So enjoy the graduations. Celebrate the family. Remember the good times you had when the children were little and you were in charge of their world. But recognize "the times, they are a changin'" for you and your children—and these no-longer-little ones must now explore the world on their own.

Dear Holy Parent, be with all parents in our world as they try to train their children in the way you would have them go. Let us all find ways to be supportive of parents and to love and respect children. Amen.

It's No Picnic

A man pumping gas next to a woman with a van load of children said to her, "Are these all your kids, or are you on a picnic?" The harried mother replied, "These are all my kids, and no, it's not a picnic."

I suppose rearing a family is always more difficult than we realize. There are mouths to feed, clothes to buy, personalities to develop, and relationships to build. There are hurts to comfort, hopes to inspire, and minds to educate as each person becomes the unique human being they were created to be. Yes, all of that is hard work.

That's why love and loyalty alone prevail as the foundation of a happy home. There are things we do for love that no money can buy. Who could afford to purchase the taxi service required to transport a child from one activity to another? What about the meals served and laundry done? And loyalty keeps us doing those things when we are tired or prefer some time alone. Family may not be a picnic but it's the hope of the world.

Help us to be loyal and loving family members, dear God. May we participate in comforting, inspiring, and educating all of your children, the hope of the world. Amen.

Bless Your Heart

"Bless your heart." My grandmother used to say that every time she laid eyes on me. She lived in the city. I lived in the country. Narrow roads and limited transportation did not make it convenient for us to get together often. But when it happened—like a visit in the summer or stopover at Christmas—it was sheer delight. My grandmother was always pleased to see me. She would turn every stone in her creative mind in an effort to grant my every wish. She would take me to special places, cook me pleasing meals, and listen to my never-ending stories of living on a farm.

It seems to me that everybody deserves a grandmother like that—one who never missed a chance to bless my heart. Most of us could use more blessing and less cursing. All of us benefit from knowing we are loved and accepted not for what we do or even for what we become. We need to be blessed simply for being who we are.

So look all around you and find someone in need. Bless somebody today. Though it is a small neighborly deed, bless somebody today.

Gracious God, you have bestowed many blessings upon us.
Use us, in turn, to be a blessing to others.
May we open our eyes to the many
opportunities we have to do so. Amen.

Gratitude

Enjoying the Trip

Do you ever take a walk with a young child? A simple trip outdoors with my three-year-old granddaughter the other day proved to be quite an adventure. She burst into the experience with abandonment and glee. She stopped and squatted down to take a closer look at the kind of things I take for granted—a rock in the road, a weed in the ditch, the tiniest of feathers shed by a bird. She seemed to care little about reaching our intended destination. She was simply enjoying the trip with a kind of curiosity that left me envious.

What happens to us goal-oriented adults that robs us of the wonder around us? Why are we so anxious to reach our destination that we cannot stop and smell the roses—or even the grass and the weeds? Do young children possess a joy of life that we have lost with the passing of time?

Questions like these flutter through my mind as I wait on my grandchild. Then I remember that someone much greater than I said, "Consider the birds of the air and the flowers of the field."

Lord, you showed us that you value children when you said, "Let the children come to me." Help us to value the child who still resides within us, that we may find more pleasure in life's simple gifts. Amen.

Bucket of Shrimp

How does a person express thanks? Eddie Rickenbacker, who lives on a beach, does it this way. Every Friday old Eddie takes a bucket of shrimp, walks down to the pier, and feeds the birds that are already waiting. You see, back in 1942, Captain Rickenbacker, with a crew of seven, was flying a B-17 on a special mission over the Pacific. They got lost, and the plane went down. All eight survived the crash, but had little hope of surviving the ocean. Then one day, as Eddie lay on his raft in quiet desperation, a bird smacked him on the face. Captain Rickenbacker managed to catch the bird, and the rest, as they say, is history. So now the old Captain, every Friday, takes his bucket of shrimp down to the pier and feeds the birds as a way of saying thanks.

How do you say thanks? We have made it, you and I. There were times when we almost didn't and times when we maybe even wished we wouldn't. But we are alive. The time is right to express our thanks.

*Loving God, time and again you provide help.
May we be open to small ways to express our gratitude
to you and to those who have been your
helping instruments in our lives. Amen.*

Wonders of the World

A group of elementary-school students were asked by their teacher to list the Seven Wonders of the World. In the allotted time, most completed an expected list: the Great Pyramids, the Taj Mahal, the Grand Canyon, the Empire State building, and so forth. One little girl, however, was having trouble. Trying to be helpful, the teacher said to the struggling student, "Why don't you read what you have so far and we will help you complete the list?"

Timidly, the little girl took her paper and started reading, "To see, to taste, to touch, to hear. But I can't decide if to laugh or to love needs to come next," lamented the little girl.

Well, there are more wonders in this world than we can quickly count. There are the wonders of springtime and harvest, the wonders of sunshine and rain. The beauty of one autumn day supersedes all the wonderful things our human hands have made. The ordinary things we take for granted like seeing, tasting, touching, smelling, and hearing may just be the greatest wonders of all. So let us pause and be grateful.

Lord of heaven and earth, we thank you for the wonders of your creation and especially for the wonders of our bodies. As we see, taste, hear, smell, and feel today, may we be grateful and may we remember to use your wondrous gifts wisely. Amen.

Thank you, IRS

Did you hear about the guy who decided to write the words "thank you" on all his checks? When he paid his mortgage, he included the words "thank you." When he paid his utility bills, he added the words "thank you." He even put the words "thank you" on his check to the IRS.

Have you learned to be thankful in all circumstances? The alarm clock disturbs your sleep, but it is a reminder that you are alive for yet another day. The gutters may need fixing and the windows cleaning, but you are thankful for a house in which to live. If we are paying extra taxes, it probably means we made more money last year than we thought we would.

I have not learned to be thankful for all circumstances. I could do without cancer, conflicts, and many other concerns of life that cause me pain. But I refuse to let my problems destroy my gratitude. So, I am trying to be thankful in all circumstances. Sometimes I am thankful for the mighty acts of God. Other times I am simply thankful that no trouble enjoys eternal life. Either way, I can be thankful.

Being thankful isn't always easy, dear God.
May we be thankful even for the troublesome
things in our lives, knowing that even in them lies
a blessing if we but open ourselves to it. Amen.

Power of Appreciation

Leadership expert Max DePree once said, "The first responsibility of a leader is to define reality. The last is to say thank you. In between the two, leader must become a servant and a debtor." How are you at the art of spreading praise? Does "thank you" flow freely from your lips, or are the words seldom spoken? People are not robots. We all have feelings and certain needs for recognition. Words of appreciation are music to our ears and energy for our souls. People who are appreciated work harder, produce more, and represent companies better than those who feel driven, demonized, or ignored.

What is true for business holds true for families too. People who live together can treat each other like furnishings to be used instead of persons to be respected. Such habits are recipes for disaster. Parents are more than taxi drivers available upon demand. Children are more than obligations to be handled without personal involvement. So just remember, praise and appreciation do more good than this world can imagine.

*Dear God how often we forget to say thank you
or speak kind words of appreciation.
May we learn to live with gratitude
and to express that gratitude often. Amen.*

Mentors

In a *Guidepost* magazine interview, actor Denzel Washington talks about the people in his past that made him the star he is today. There was the director of the boy's club that taught Denzel to dream. There was the neighborhood barber that taught him to serve others. There was the acting coach that taught him to believe in himself. Well, the list goes on, but you get the idea.

No one of us is a self-made person. Whatever we are and whatever we may become are a compilation of tunes played upon our violin of life by significant others. There have been friends and relatives, teachers and counselors, neighbors and even strangers who have contributed to the persons we are today. Such knowledge is a reason to rejoice. It is also a call to humility. The arrogance of thinking we did it our way is at best an illusion. Sure, we've made a few choices and decisions. Many of us have had to work for what we have, to sacrifice for what we have accomplished, but we did not do it alone. We have had mentors along the way who made a difference. Maybe it's time we expressed our gratitude to these significant people, past and present.

*Thank you, dear God, for all of the people who have
helped us along the way. Help us to recognize
that we too are mentors to others.
We pray for your guidance and wisdom. Amen.*

Gratitude in the Night

Inside Edition anchor, Deborah Norville, was in town last week to tell us that thankfulness helps us live happier, healthier lives. The science of gratitude really works, according to Deborah. Of course, biblical writers have been saying that for more than two-thousand years. As one suggests, "Give thanks in all circumstances, for this is God's will for you."

An attitude of gratitude is good for body, mind, and soul. It activates the brain, stimulates the mind, and soothes the soul. Do you live a life of gratitude?

Oh, I know, there are circumstances that trouble us, people that bother us, dreams that escape us. One person put this note on their refrigerator: "Dear God, I know you said you would never give me more than I could handle. I just wish you didn't trust me so much."

Yes, life can be tough, troublesome, temporary. But never let the trials of the day steal your gratitude at night. You are alive. You are not alone. You will overcome. So, as we used to say in the country, "Keep on keeping on." It will do you a world of good.

You are generous, dear God. Let us awake each morning with gratitude in our hearts. At the end of each day, Lord, may we look back and thank you for your blessing both great and small that we have encountered. Amen.

What Might Have Been

What might have been? Do you ever ask that question? A British journalist wrote a book a few years ago asking what might have been had some major moments of history turned out differently. What if Napoleon had not met his Waterloo? What if Great Britain had won the War of Independence? And what if the Japanese had not attacked Pearl Harbor? While the list goes on, the question remains: What might have been?

I sometimes ask that question about my personal life too. Do you? What might have been had I taken a different job, made some different choices, followed a different path? Of course, that was then, and we can't go back again. Nevertheless, all of us nearly miss the things we get and almost get the things we miss. That's life.

So I stop from time to time to thank God for being at work in all things for the good of humanity. God takes the good, the bad, and the ugly and weaves it into something meaningful, helpful, and eternal.

Dear God, we are grateful that your Holy Spirit works among us. May we focus beyond all the "what ifs" so that we can be open to ways you can use us for the good of your earthly kingdom. Amen.

One-Word Description

More and more, the singular word that describes my approach to life is the word "gratitude." I am grateful for the gift of life. I am grateful for a host of friends. I am grateful for my family. I am grateful for my freedom. I am grateful.

One of the special blessings of my present life is that of grandparenting. Grandchildren put us in touch with a simple wonder and joy that is easily forgotten in the complexities of making a living and meeting the demands of the day. When our five-year-old grandson visits, he always insists on saying the blessing for our meals. While he has several selections in his repertoire of prayers, he most often bursts forth singing these words: "O, the Lord's been good to me, and so I thank the Lord, for giving me the things I need, the sun, the rain, and the apple seed. O, the Lord's been good to me."

Whether or not we are aware of it, the Lord's been good to all of us. God has helped us carry every burden. Our every sorrow God has shared. Whether our days have been sunny or dreary, God has been there beside us to hold us and guide us.

O you, Lord, have been good to me,
and so I thank you, Lord, for giving me the things I need,
the sun, the rain, and the apple seed.
O you, Lord, have been good to me." Amen.

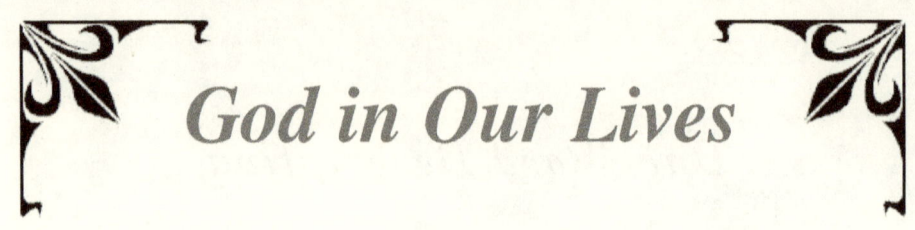

God in Our Lives

Is God Missing?

Ben and Sam were brothers and were a problem for everyone, especially their mother. Finally, the exasperated mother sent Sam to see the minister, hoping he might straighten him out. The pastor greeted Sam warmly, but hardly knowing what to do, finally asked the boy the first question in the catechism which is, "Where is God?"

Sam didn't say a word. The reverend asked Sam again, a little more sternly, "Where is God?"

Sam persisted in his silence. Seeing he was not about to get through to the Sam, the pastor told him to go on home. Arriving home, Sam immediately ran up the stairs to his brother's room. "Ben," whispered Sam, "we are really in trouble now. God is missing and they think we had something to do with it."

If God is missing in our lives, maybe we do have something to do with it. God is the same yesterday, today, and forever. God is not watching us from a distance, but coming to us in the present moment, touching us gently with his grace.

Always wise and present God, you never move away,
but we often try to moveaway from you.
Help us to know that we can only be the people
you call us to be when we are touched by your grace.
May we be always present to you. Amen.

Bigger Is Better?

In a Tom Wilson cartoon, Ziggy is taking a look at his long shadow in the sun. Pleased with what he sees, Ziggy makes this comment: "Even the little guy can cast a big shadow once he's found his place in the sun!" I like that attitude; how about you?

We are tempted daily to glorify the large and succumb to the power of the big. We have big houses, big shopping centers, big convention centers, and even big churches. Americans have adopted the idea that bigger is better. The mantra of business these days is merger, to become bigger in order to be successful in the competitive market place.

Why is bigger better? Is it not our task to find our place in the sun and cast our shadow whatever its size might be? Comparisons pale in the light of the universe. I sat in a planetarium recently with my grandson, amazed again at the vastness of space and the minuteness of Earth. Yet, God has taken us specks on this tiny planet and accomplished great things.

*God of the universe, thank you for loving us and caring for us,
as tiny as we are in the vastness of your realm.
Help us not to judge ourselves by the world's standards
but to value even the small things we do because they are
important in your eyes. Amen.*

Holding Our Breath

I watched a child the other day throw a temper tantrum in the grocery store. Something about the Cheerios and the Frosted Flakes upset him. At first he screamed to the top of his voice in the sure and certain hope that his mother would be embarrassed and let him have his way. Instead, she ignored him. That's when the child decided to stop breathing. His face turned red; his lips turned purple. Perhaps he thought someone would call 911. Instead, his mother went on shopping. Out of scare tactics, the little boy decided to straighten up.

As I left that grocery store, I began thinking how I often interact with God like that little boy. When things don't go my way, I get mad at God. I throw a temper tantrum. I scream his name in vain, hoping to get his attention. Then I decide to hold my spiritual breath. I announce to the world that God is absent when in reality God is closer than the air I breathe. In my rebellion, I make an important discovery. God is to the soul what oxygen is to the body—absolutely essential!

We so often think we can get along without you, God,
but then events in our lives show us how essential you are.
May we remember that our souls always need you. Thank you
for loving us even when we seem to stop loving you. Amen.

Coincidences?

What I assumed to be coincidences on the treadmills of time, I am now reconsidering to be "God-incidences" on the course of life. Week after week, I plant a thought on the airwaves without the slightest knowledge of who may be listening, needing, or responding to anything I may have to say. Then it happens. Somebody drops me an e-mail, stops me in the grocery store, or flags me down at a ballgame to say the encouragement was just what they needed at that moment. Walt Whitman used to say miracles are happening around us all the time. We just need eyes to see, ears to hear, and souls to absorb their reality.

Several weeks ago, I was in ancient Corinth searching for a small place to hold a Christian worship service. I found a shade tree, a few benches, and two Asian women enjoying their lunch. I asked permission to invade their privacy only to discover they were members of a sister United Methodist church in Singapore. This spontaneous fellowship enriched our whole visit to this historic Christian site. So let us stay alert to the "God-incidences" of our lives.

*Dear God, open our eyes to your action in our daily lives.
Let us be more appreciative of the "God-incidences" all around us,
and may our faith increase as we recognize them.
Thank you for all of your "God-incidences." Amen.*

Tsunami

Sooner or later somebody had to ask the question. Then it appeared on the editorial page of *The Tennessean*. Columnist David Brooks put it in print—"Was it the wrath of God or just nature's lottery?" The question of course referred to the horrific destruction of human life caused by the tsunami in Southern Asia. The suffering is more than any of us can imagine, even with frontline views on the television and Internet. And sensible people want to know, "Where is God when disaster strikes?" The adjoining cartoon even pressed the point further. Humans excelled at war, terrorism, and other acts of destruction in 2004. But all of this seemed like the pale actions of amateurs compared to Mother Nature's tsunami.

If we must have someone to blame, God is probably more capable of handling our anger than anyone. So if you need to give him a piece of your mind, go ahead. God already knows what you are thinking anyway. But don't stop there. In every disaster, God is working for good. See the nations sending aid. See the world religions uniting in relief efforts. See neighbors helping neighbors. God is in all of those responses too.

O compassionate God, may we see you at work among people suffering in the aftermath of natural disasters. Show us how we can witness to your presence in our response to human need. Amen.

A Little Help

I watched a father and daughter leaving the bank the other day. The little girl ran ahead of her dad to open the heavy door. She huffed and puffed and pushed to no avail. Then she stepped back and started again, this time pushing with all her might. To her delight, the door swung open, and she marched out victorious. Of course, the little girl was oblivious to the fact that her father had his hand on the door far above her head the second time around.

What a lesson for life! All of us can use a little help with the doors of our lives. Sometimes we can use a lot. As we push and shove our way along the crowded corridors of our days, we run into obstacles that are too hard and too heavy to manage alone. In times like these, we are wise to remember that we are not alone.

So lean on God when you're not strong. God will be your friend. God will help you carry on. Like a loving father, God is more anxious to help than we are to ask. And the next time some door of opportunity opens to your surprise, you might look up and thank the One who was helping all the time.

You are always there to help us, dear Lord.
Let us not be too afraid to ask for your help
or too impatient to await your guidance.
Thank you for helping all the time. Amen.

Life's Uncertainties

In a Tom Wilson cartoon, Ziggy is standing at a shopping mall directional sign. "You are here," says the sign with a big red arrow and a big round dot. Underneath, somebody has made this addition: "But who knows where you'll be tomorrow?"

Uncertainty is a fact of life, is it not? Change comes quickly in our kind of world. Some news can be disturbing, like a bad report from your doctor or a dismissal from your employer. Other news can be rewarding, like an unexpected promotion or a brand new opportunity. Who knows what a day may hold?

That's why it's important to view life as an adventure—not one darn thing after another, but one challenge after another. No trouble enjoys eternal life. Every problem has a lifespan. And new opportunities force us to grow, develop, and expand into the people we never dreamed we could be.

So you know what? I'm learning to go with the flow. There are many things about tomorrow that I will never understand. But I know God holds tomorrow. And I know God holds my hand.

You hold us in the palm of your hand, dear Lord.
Even during difficult times, show us new opportunities to grow
into the people you created us to be.
You hold tomorrow. Amen.

Closer than We Think

You'll never know that God is all you need until God is all you have. I've been thinking a lot about that old statement lately. It's one thing to trust in God when life is together and all our support systems are in place. In times like these, faith comes easy. But what happens when life falls through the cracks? When we try and fail? When our dreams are shattered? When our investments crash? When the health we have taken for granted disappears like a thief in the night? Where is God in times like these?

Maybe God is closer than we think. Oh, I know, trouble can separate us from God and cause us to question our beliefs. But trouble doesn't have to do that. Trouble can help us make a closer connection between the divine in us and the God of the universe. We will never know that God is all we need until God is all we have. So take it from me. I have touched the bottom, and the bottom is sound. I have stared death in the face and found I was not alone. I have walked through the valley and discovered God to be with me.

Dear God, you give us what we need.
You restore our souls and bring us peace.
You are with us during our most difficult times.
Thank you, Shepherd God, for caring for us. Amen.

When We Fail

Nearly a millennium ago, the people of the tiny village of Pisa, Italy, built a bell tower to complete the major construction of a holy site known as Miracle Square. The eager builders, however, made a crucial mistake while constructing the foundation of the tower. In just a few years after construction, the tower began to lean. Some thought it would fall, but it didn't. Some thought it ought to be torn down, but the town leaders wouldn't. The result is what we know today as the Leaning Tower of Pisa, which attracts thousands of visitors daily and has been featured in the music videos of Janet Jackson and the movie *Superman III*.

As I waded through the crowd recently to get a personal glimpse of this world-renowned mistake, I stood for a moment to ponder what God might do with the faults and failures of our lives. None of us get it right all the time. We falter. We fail. We get so anxious to build our lives that we neglect the foundation. But let us not be dismayed. God can use broken pottery, leaning towers, and our feeble lives for the inspiration of others.

*Gracious God, you forgive us when we do wrong.
You help us to learn from our failures.
You provide us with new opportunities to grow as people of faith
who work for good in your world. Thank you for all of that,
and may we open ourselves to you in our lives. Amen.*

Nervous Wreck

Two mothers were talking over coffee about their teenage daughters. One mother lamented, "My daughter doesn't tell me anything. I'm a nervous wreck."

The other mother immediately chimed in saying, "My daughter tells me everything. I'm a nervous wreck."

However we slice it, life contains enough worries to make us feel like nervous wrecks. There are bills to pay, jobs to keep, and most of all, children to rear. We go to sleep worried and wake up with problems on our mind. Some of us are doing graduate work at the University of Anxiety.

A wise teacher long ago made a poignant point by asking the question, "Which of you, by worrying about it, can add a single hour to your life? Or who of you by fretting about it can stretch your stature even an inch?"

It's something to ponder, isn't it—not to stimulate more worry, but to bring us release and peace.

*Dear God, may we make time to rest
in the peace you offer us so that
the sense of your presence with us
carries over into our more stress-filled times. Amen.*

Finding God

Most spiritual seekers think they have to get away to some monastery, retreat center, or anywhere but where they happen to be at the present moment to find God. But Bonnie Miller-McLemore, a wife, mother, author, and professor, has a better idea. Like Brother Lawrence of old, Bonnie finds God in the routines of the day—in hellos and good-byes, in the baths and stories of children, in the chores and laundry of the household.

Do you do that? Do you encounter the Holy in the midst of the mundane? Do you feel the presence of God in your everyday work and play? God is everywhere. God inhabits holy places and makes Himself known in the heavens. Even when we are going through hell, God leads his dear children along. Best of all, God is present in the ordinary too. When days bring neither ecstasies nor emergencies, God is there to comfort and guide.

*Open our eyes, dear God, that we may see
signs of your presence all around us, even in the
most ordinary tasks and encounters.
Help us not to forget your ever-presence
so that we find joy and peace
in our daily comings and goings. Amen.*

 # Our Nation

Immigration

When the Europeans immigrated to North America, they were not sent home. Instead, the government gave sections of land in the West to anyone who would move there and homestead it. Thousands of people left the cities and, for the first time in their lives, had property to call their own. Self-reliance was the watchword, and a pioneer with an axe in one hand and a rifle in the other became the national hero.

I do not pretend to know the answer to present problems with immigration. Obviously, something needs to be done. But let us be wise, lest, trying to better the matter, we wind up making things worse. Of this I am certain: all humans deserve respect. All persons have rights. Red and yellow, black and white, Asian, African, Jew, or Latino, whatever our class, whatever our creed, we are all loved children of God. So let this be our moral compass as we chart the course of our future. Let that great American motto of "freedom and justice for all" be our guiding light.

*O God, as we make political decisions
and personal ones, help us to see everyone
around us as your children
and to love them because you love us. Amen.*

Prayer for Our Country

A man took his son to Washington and watched from the gallery as the House came to order and the chaplain led in prayer. After the Amen, the boy turned to his dad and asked, "Why did the minister pray for all those people?" The father quickly responded, "He didn't. He took one look at all those people and prayed for our country."

Whatever your political persuasion, I suspect we would all be wise to be in prayer for our country. Our great ideal of "liberty and justice for all" is not something to be taken for granted in the hands of fallible people. The best public leaders make mistakes. Some stoop to shocking compromises for personal gain. All need divine wisdom and guidance.

It will take unusual integrity and unfaltering faith for any leader to pursue the common good. So may God once more bless America. America is great because America is good. If we cease to be good, we will cease to be great!

Dear God of all nations, help our nation be the nation we profess to be—one nation under God with liberty and justice for all. May we open our hearts and minds to what this means for us both as citizens of our nation but above all as citizens of your kingdom. Amen.

Idolatry

I can appreciate the culture wars going on in America these days between those who want to wipe every reference to God out of our society and those who want to turn our country into a theocracy. Any nation that cannot depend on some absolute moral foundation is destined to corruption.

On the other hand, have those who insist on placing the Ten Commandments in public places at any cost betrayed the second commandment they seek to protect? As I recall, the Second Commandment instructs us not to make for ourselves any graven images or idols, lest we wind up worshiping the image of God instead of the living God. So I have to ask this question: Have the stone tablets on which the commandments are written become idols? Have political maneuvers to keep them posted become a kind of idol worship?

I know no easy answers to present culture struggles, but I must ask, "What is liberty and justice for all? What is one nation under God?"

*Dear God, because there are no easy answers
to our present culture struggles,
Help us to recognize the idols we worship,
O God, so that we worship only you. Amen.*

Left Behind

Tim LaHaye and Jerry Jenkins have wowed the world with a series of apocalyptic novels concerning the last days of life on this planet. The evangelistic appeal of these novels is to get right with God so you won't be left behind.

There are people in America who are already being left behind. Their souls may be ready, but their bodies and spirits are sagging with the weight of life and the growing lack of opportunity to pursue personal dreams. The divide between the haves and the have-nots is deep and becoming deeper in America. A growing percentage of our population is literally and tragically being left behind. Martin Luther King, Jr., once said, "No nation can be great if it does not have concern for the least of these."

I am concerned about eternal salvation. All of us need to be ready to walk in Jerusalem just like John. We must also be willing to care for the least and the lost, those left behind. It might affect our eternal destination more than we realize.

Dear Jesus, in your parable you taught us that whatever we do or fail to do to for the least among us we do or fail to do for you. Open our eyes to the needs around us so that we do not leave any behind.. Amen.

Hate

According to the Associated Press, a plan to build a mosque in the Houston suburb of Katy, Texas, has triggered a neighborhood dispute with community members warning the place will become a terrorist hotbed. One adjoining property owner, Mr. Craig Baker, is threatening to hold pig races on Fridays to offend the Muslims. The pig race plan ran into problems however when Mr. Baker discovered that Muslims don't hate pigs; they just don't eat them. Mr. Baker still plans to go on with his pig races. He is quoted as saying, "I would be like a total idiot if I didn't."

While we might debate the nature of a total idiot, hate continues to be alive and well in this country. Fear has driven us to be suspicious of anyone who might be a different color, a different religion, or a different sexual orientation than I. We have become experts at categorizing and demonizing people instead of treating people as children of God worthy of love and respect. Isn't it time we learned to live together as brothers and sisters before we perish apart as fools?

Dear God, help us to be a nation of people who love instead of hate, people who work together for the good of the whole rather than create divisiveness to protect our own self-interest. Help us to understand that this is what a nation that proclaims to be under God does. Amen.

Greed or God's Will?

Albert Einstein once said, "We cannot solve the problems we have created with the same thinking that created them." As I ponder the problem of health care in America, and particularly the Tenn-care problem in Tennessee, I wonder if we would be wise to follow the advice of Einstein.

Health care in America has become a huge for-profit business. Drug companies and insurance companies exercise considerable control over government policies. The days when hospitals and retirement communities were operated by religious organizations motivated by compassion to serve have passed away.

What would happen if we replaced greed with good will in the medical industry of our day? What difference would it make if people became as cautious about spending insurance dollars as they are their own dollars? Can any business survive without integrity as a core value of providers and consumers? Maybe it's time to solve old problems with a new way of thinking.

Dear God, the Great Healer, you call us to provide opportunities for healing for all of God's children. May greed and concern for profit not take precedence over your call. Amen.

Cleaning Up America

It was one of those clean-up-your neighborhood days. As I drove along, I spotted a little boy, maybe eight years of age or so, pulling a plastic bag behind him filled with trash. Moved by the sight, I stopped, rolled down my window and said to the kid "What are you doing?" He didn't know me from Adam, but with bold confidence he replied, "Mister, I'm cleaning up America!"

Now that kid had a noble purpose in life. He was cleaning up America in a literal sense by removing the litter from the roads. For the sake of me, I don't understand why people trash our streets and highways with stuff thrown from their cars. I see signs threatening fines, but I have never known a person arrested for the crime.

Of course, there are other highways that are being trashed with filth too. The Internet highway is a prime example. This marvelous invention for information has brought with it the constant bombardment of pornography, including the exploitation of children. Maybe it's time to clean up America!

Dear Creator God, may we be good and unselfish stewards of this beautiful planet Earth that you gave us for our home. May we also be good stewards of our bodies and minds, for we have been created in your image. Amen.

In God We Trust

The year was 1861. Our country was engaged in a bitter civil war. Treasury Secretary Salmon P. Chase sent this letter to James Pollock. "No nation can be strong except in the strength of God, or safe except in his defense." With that, Mr. Chase proposed the words "In God We Trust" be inscribed on all our national coins. It was later added to our currency. And in 1956, the Congress of the United States made "In God We Trust" our national motto. The slogan continues to survive in spite of those who protest that God cannot be trusted and has no place in statements of government.

What does it mean for a nation to trust in God? Does it mean that God is on our side when we find ourselves in conflicts around the world? Hardly! Does it mean that we are the favorites of the Lord—that God loves us more than he loves others? I doubt that! To trust God means to humble ourselves in the presence of the Almighty. To trust God means to seek God's will and follow God's ways. Maybe it's time to trust in God.

*O God of Power and Might, may our nation trust
in your power and might and not its own.
May we recognize that your power and might come with
love, grace, and forgiveness so that we live out
those qualities in our national lives. Amen.*

Peace

On Center Stage: Fear and Hate

Author Wendell Berry makes this observation in one of his essays, "Thoughts in the Presence of Fear": "In a time such as this, when we have been seriously and most cruelly hurt by those who hate us, and when we must consider ourselves to be gravely threatened by those same people, it is hard to speak of the ways of peace and to remember that Christ enjoined us to love our enemies, but this is no less necessary for being difficult."

Could Mr. Berry be right? Fear and hate seem to have taken center stage in America these days. They show up in public pronouncements and casual conversations. No one can board an airplane without being made consciously aware of the danger involved from people who hate us. Legislatures debate the extent the government must go to guarantee the safety of its citizens. Even six years after that frightful day of September 11, we are constantly warned to be careful, for all this might very well happen again.

Are fear and hate simply signs of the times, or can we find a better way? Can we be secure without demonizing people who are different from us? Can we be safe without developing prisons of our own making? Such are the challenges of our time!

You taught peace, dear God, but we practice war.
Help us to turn from hate to love, from fear to trust,
knowing that if we but listen to the God we profess,
God will guide our nation down the right path. Amen.

Casualties of War

Erwin Kowalke from Hammer, Germany, has spent his whole life digging for bones—the vertebrae, the teeth, and crushed skulls of soldiers who lost their lives in World War II. So far he has collected 1,968 bones. Each one is carefully marked and placed in a box. A reporter asked Erwin why he would spend his whole life searching for abandoned remains. The forty-three-year veteran bone searcher replied by saying, "In these bones, you see what war is like. I know war now. I'll tell you what it is. War is young men killing other young men they do not know on the orders of old men who know one another too well."

Casualties of present-day wars are no longer just young men. They are young women, and a growing number of innocent children as well. But they are still too often young people killing young people they don't know on the orders of old men and women who cannot learn to get along with each other.

I have a feeling that if we sent the rich and famous, along with powerful politicians, into hand-to-hand combat, wars would cease much sooner.

*Dear Jesus, you said to love our enemies
and to pray for those who persecute us.
We find that hard to do. Open our minds and hearts
to your way in the world so that our first response
is peace and not war. Amen.*

Prayer for Peace

I read in the paper the other day about three-million Muslims raising their hands in prayer for global peace. The prayers concluded a three-day Islamic meeting in Tongi, Bangladesh. As my mind tried to fathom three-million people united in prayer in one place, a dream arose in my heart. What if people of good will around the world united in prayer for peace? What if Buddhists and Hindus, Muslims and Christians, each in their own way, became prayerful about peace?

As my heart pursued the idea, my cynical self kicked into gear. The religions of the world are not united in anything. Why would they unite in prayer? The Christians of the world would rather argue theology than talk with God. Where could you find three-million Christians who would lift their hands in prayer? There are about twenty-five-million United Methodists scattered around the world. We are more united in our name than we are in spirit. Then it really hit me. How often do I pray for global peace? And what am I willing to do about it?

*O Lord, help us to wake us each morning
with peace in our hearts and on our minds
so that, daily, we pray for peace
in your beloved world. Amen.*

Have We Forgotten?

Because we humans are often forgetful, we need a day to remember. We need a day to be thankful. Our culture, maybe more than any other, tends to bury its dead and soon forget them. We are so busy embracing the future that we forget the past and its impact on the present.

So, I ask us all: have we forgotten? Have we forgotten our fathers and mothers who forged the way and sacrificed so much that we could enjoy our way of life? Have we forgotten? Have we forgotten the high price of freedom and the cherished privilege that is ours to live in this land of the free and the home of the brave? Have we forgotten? Have we forgotten our blessings in our surge for more possessions? Have we forgotten the value of friendship, the joy of family, the privilege of meaningful employment—not to mention the sheer gift of life?

It's time to remember. Remember and be thankful. Remember and be grateful. Remember and live meaningfully so that those who come behind us will find us faithful.

*Dear God of many gifts, sometimes
we lose track of our true blessings.
Today and every day, may we remember
to give you thanks. Amen.*

Life and Death

A videotaped message left in the rubble in Madrid following those devastating series of bombs on commuter trains left this explanation: "You love life and we love death!" Certainly the message is frightening, and we hardly know how to defend ourselves against it. We find ourselves in a different kind of war. It is a conflict of ideals. It is a terror of principles. It is an all-out attack on human dignity. In some strange way, do we wind up playing into the hand of the enemy by taking up traditional arms and sophisticated weapons only to be stunned by those more than willing to sacrifice themselves for the cause?

Is this a war that must be won by common-sense people of all religions, nationalities, and creeds joining together for the survival of humanity? A resurgent and profound spiritual vitality is our greatest defense against the nihilism of fear and death. Somehow sober-minded people who believe in life must quell this death knoll that is stealing our souls.

*Dear Lord of all, are we listening to our enemies
more than we are listening to you?
Please forgive us if that is true
and renew in us your desire for
trust, respect, and peace. Amen.*

Count Your Blessings

In a *Peanuts* cartoon, Lucy laments, "My life is a drag. I'm completely fed up. I've never felt so low in my life."

That's when her little brother Linus says, "Try to think of things you're thankful for. Count your blessings."

But Lucy is not about to give in to such encouragement. "I could count my blessings on one finger," she asserts. "I never had anything, never will have anything. I don't get half the breaks that other people do. You want me to count my blessings. What have I to be thankful for?"

"Well," insists Linus, "for one thing, you have a little brother that loves you."

Most of us do not have to look very far to find something for which to be thankful. Blessings abound. Morning by morning, there are new mercies in our midst. All we have needed, God has provided.

I know it's not always an easy road. We have mountains to climb and obstacles to overcome. Even in the midst of life's challenges, we discover strength we never knew we had and grace to carry on. So let us give thanks!

You have given us so much, O God,
yet when something goes wrong,
how we can forget your blessing upon us!
May we be a thankful people. Amen.

In Harm's Way

Whenever we pause to celebrate our freedom, let us not forget the men and women who are giving their lives in military service around the world. They are on the front lines of combat in Iraq and Afghanistan. They are answering the calls of state and nation in homeland defense. They are keeping America safe at home and abroad.

Whatever our opinion about the present war, let us never hesitate to honor our heroes. They have put their lives on hold. They are separated from family and friends. They live in harm's way. Some are dying in combat and others are being critically wounded. As we go our merry ways, living our normal lives, they are experiencing nothing normal. Let us never forget or take their service for granted.

May people of all faiths unite in a concerted prayer for peace. May the God of all grace forgive our foolish ways. May the Lord of all nations teach us the fine art of sharing instead of shooting, helping instead of hating, loving instead of leveraging power, lest we all perish in our selfish pursuits.

You have called us, O God, to beat sword into plowshares,
but we continue to turn to war as a solution.
Please forgive us for our warring ways and open our
minds and hearts to peaceful solutions.
We pray that you watch over those in harm's way. Amen.

Outer Obnoxiousness

In a *Peanuts* cartoon, Lucy laments to Charlie Brown, "I hate everything. I hate everybody. I hate the whole wide world."

Charlie Brown replies, "I thought you had inner peace."

"I do," snaps Lucy, "but I have outer obnoxiousness."

Do you ever run into people like that?

Some people are born in the objective case. They wear a chip on their shoulder and simply hate whatever happens around them. They even seem to gain some personal satisfaction from their persistent protest. They may have inner peace, but they make life miserable for those around them.

Whatever the psychological ramifications of our contrariness, we are called to do better than that. As far as it's possible, we must try to live at peace with all people. So the next time you are tempted to hate everybody and everything, stop, step back, and take a more realistic look at the world. Others will benefit from your thoughtfulness.

*Dear Lord of all, help us to have
both inner and outer peace.
When we are tempted to be contrary,
remind us to live peacefully in your world. Amen.*

Tiny Bird

A local library offered a community contest for the best painting symbolizing peace. When the judges reviewed the entries, they narrowed the paintings down to two.

One painting portrayed a majestic lake, so tranquil and still that the lush hills behind it were perfectly mirrored in its reflection. A blue sky was overhead. Wildflowers bloomed along the shore. Deer could be seen grazing in the meadow. It was a picture of peace.

The second painting was much different. It portrayed a terrible storm, winds blowing, trees bending, debris flying through the air. But perched on one of those twisted limbs was a tiny bird. Observers were led to believe the bird was singing.

Which of these two paintings would you have selected as a picture of peace? The judges went for the bird. Peace is not the absence of conflict. It is assurance in the midst of conflict.

Lord, bring assurance to those in war-torn areas.
Be with those of us who are losing hope that wars will cease.
Finally, bless the peacemakers with courage and strength of
conviction that one day their voice will be heard. Amen.

Enemies

It's been said that if you want to kill your enemies, it's best to kill them twice. Take away their humanity by demonizing them and then drop the bombs into their bunkers. I suspect that saying is true.

We continue to live in a world at war. In this elongated conflict, we will be wise to clearly define the enemy. Terrorists are our enemy, whatever their color or creed, whatever their nationality or religion. We need to keep that clear in our minds. We are not engaged in a Holy War between Christians and Muslims. We are not in conflict with peace-abiding citizens from the Middle East. Ordinary Muslims, wherever they live, do not deserve our rage. They are people like you and me who want to make a living and raise a family in the midst of great upheaval.

War does strange things to people. Fear causes us to generalize and hypothesize. If one person is evil, then all of his kind must be evil too. Such thinking is just not true.

So let us take a second look. Let us respect all people. Let us learn to live together as brothers and sisters before we perish apart as fools.

Dear Jesus, the bringer of peace that passes understanding, teach us to see others as you see them. May we respect others whom we consider to be different from us. Help us to replace fear with trust in you. Amen.

Battle for the Heart

General Omar Bradley recently said, "The world has achieved brilliance without wisdom and power without conscience. Ours is a world of nuclear giants and ethical infants."

As tensions between countries on this planet continue to mount and threats become a way of life, we are going to need leaders that are wise and willing to make mature, ethical decisions. Survival is not about power; it's about conscience. It is about doing the right thing at the right time for the common good. World community is not about threats of nuclear destruction, but about a conversation around how we may learn to live together with our differences lest we perish apart as fools.

Our present war is not about guns and bombs. It is much deeper than that. It is a fight for the hearts and minds of people around the world. It could very easily deteriorate into a religious war if, in fact, it has not already done so. The battle for the heart will not be won with swords' loud clashing. It will be won with deeds of love and mercy that has the power to gain the respect of decent people everywhere.

Almighty God, give our leaders the wisdom and courage to find solutions other than war, Help each one of us in our corner of the world to become a part of the conversation about living peacefully. Amen.

Prayer

Directly to the Lord

In a *Family Circus* cartoon, Billy is trying to pray his way through a thunderstorm. Sitting in the middle of the bed, with his hands folded, Billy offers this prayer: "It's okay, Lord, to take pictures in the dark, but don't grumble so loud when they don't turn out."

Do you know what I like about that prayer? Prayer is straightforward and to the point. It doesn't beat around the bush or cover its concern with a lot of flowery words. Billy just takes his concern directly to the Lord and leaves it there.

Do you have a prayer life like that? Is your relationship with God strong enough that you can speak your mind without threatening your friendship? People in the Bible not only praised the Lord, they argued with the Lord, pleaded with the Lord. They let the Lord know what they felt and thought.

Such confrontations of wills are not signs of weak faith, but witnesses to strong faith, faith that stands the storm, including the thundering that comes with it.

O God, help us to remember that you are compassionate. You understand our problems, sorrows, anxieties, and anger. May we be willing to express them to you so that, together, we can make it through the storms to a more peaceful time with you. Amen.

Still in Bed?

I found a prayer the other day that I want to share with you.

"So far today, God, I've done all right. I haven't gossiped, haven't lost my temper, haven't been greedy, grumpy, nasty, selfish, overindulgent, or told anyone to mind their own business and stay out of mine. I'm really glad about that. But in a few minutes, Lord, I'm going to get out of bed, and from then on, I'm going to need a lot of help."

Because most of us need a lot of help, we pray. We pray for wisdom and guidance, for strength and health, for grace and forgiveness, and rightly so. God is in the forgiving, helping, healing business. Prayer is the grand acknowledgment that life has its confrontation. Prayer is leaning on the everlasting arms, learning from somebody who sees things clearer than you and I. Have you left your room this morning? Did you think to pray?

*Dear God, let me begin and end each day
with a conversation with you.
During the in-between times,
help me remember that you are present
to our needs and concerns. Amen.*

Worry

It's been said that worry is like a rocking chair. It gives you something to do, but it doesn't get you anywhere. Have you thought about that? Certainly all of us have some worries. We have children to rear, bills to pay, relationships to maintain, and careers to pursue. These things, and countless other things, cause us concern.

It is possible, however, for normal concern to evolve into chronic anxiety. Because we humans can remember the past, anticipate the future, and make choices about the present, our worries can pile up on us, robbing us of joy and causing great personal harm.

So when I get bogged down with worry, I reach for a prayer that Reinhold Niebuhr taught us to pray, saying, "God, grant me the serenity to accept the things I cannot change; courage to change the things I can; and wisdom to know the difference."

All of us worry, dear Lord—some of us more than others.
Help us to remember the lilies of the field,
that Solomon in all his glory was not arrayed like one of them.
May we put our trust and faith in you, God,
that you love us and will care for us. Amen.

Ice Cream

As a family gathered for a meal in a local restaurant, the six-year-old son asked to say the blessing. As everyone bowed their heads, the boy said, "God is great. God is good. Could we have some ice cream with this food? Amen." The family smiled, but a woman sitting nearby took offense. "That's what's wrong with America," she snorted. "Kids today don't even know how to pray." The boy, who couldn't help but hear, began to cry.

Thank you, God, that there was an elderly man in the restaurant who came to the rescue. He walked over, laid his hand on the boy's shoulder, and said "I happen to know that God thought that was a great prayer. And furthermore, ice cream is sometimes good for the soul."

The boy finished his meal and got a sundae. But instead of eating it himself, he took it over to the woman and said, "Here, this is for you. Sometimes ice cream is good for the soul, and I think your soul could use a little help."

Dear God, whenever our souls need help,
may we turn to you. Let us never judge another's prayers,
for every prayer and the person praying it
are precious to you. Amen.

Prayer for the Day

Consider offering this prayer to get you through the day:

Lord, keep me from the habit of thinking I must say something on every subject under the sun. Release me from the craving to straighten out everybody's affairs. Keep me free from confusion and give me wings to get to the point. I ask for grace enough to listen to the tales of others' pains and patience enough to endure my own.

Teach me the glorious lesson that occasionally I may be mistaken, even downright wrong. Give me the ability to see good things in unexpected places and talents in unexpected people. And give me, O Lord, the grace to tell them so.

Make me thoughtful but not moody, helpful but not bossy, patient but not pouting. Give me a little something to forgive each day that I may grow in understanding your unlimited forgiveness of me. And may I walk softly and tread gently around the lives of all your children, making today count and anxiety about tomorrow cease.

With a prayer like that in the depths of your heart, you can make every day a good day.

*Dear Lord, sometimes we may think
it's wrong to pray for ourselves.
Help us to know that you are waiting to help us
during even our most ordinary of days. Amen.*

If Your Knees Are Shaking

When your knees are shaking, try kneeling on them! That's what Abraham Lincoln did. "I often go to my knees," said Lincoln, "because I have no place else to go." During the turbulence and turmoil of the Civil War, when families were killing their own kin, Lincoln needed wisdom and strength beyond himself. He found it through prayer.

Life has a way of asking from us what we fear is not in us. The demands are heavy. The decisions are deep. The struggles are serious. The temptations are strong. The fear is real. All of us need some help sometime. Wise leaders know their help comes from the Lord. The one who keeps us neither slumbers nor sleeps. God has a toll free number. You can call anytime.

So if your knees are shaking, try kneeling on them. It can make all the difference.

*May we know that you are with us
during our most difficult times,
loving God. Calm our shaking knees and
let us entrust our concerns with you. Amen.*

Lost

Brennan Hawkins, an eleven-year-old Boy Scout, got lost in a rugged Utah wilderness. A volunteer searcher finally found Brennan four days later, cold, wet, a little dehydrated, and very hungry. The shy boy was asked by the inquisitive media what he did first when he discovered he was lost. The boy paused for a moment and then said softly "I prayed."

In one way or another, I suspect all of us get lost from time to time. Life can seem like a maze that has no easy entrances or exits. So, we wander here and there, encountering more dead-ends than thoroughfares. In times like these, we need some help to find our way home. We need friends and family who will search for us. We need the peace and presence of God to make it through the day and comfort us through the night. When we are lost, it is a pretty good idea to pray.

The God of all wisdom will not leave us in the wilderness alone. He rejoices in finding lost people. So, the next time you don't know which way to turn, do what the Boy Scout did. Pray!

O God, thank you for never leaving us in the wilderness alone.
Help us to pay attention to all the ways
we can become lost and open ourselves to your
wise and patient guidance. Amen.

Prayer

In a *Family Circus* cartoon, Dolly is saying her bedtime prayers. As she prays, she begins to wonder how this thing called prayer really works. So Dolly stops, looks up to her mom, and asks, "Just how many prayers can God listen to at once?"

There are mysteries to prayer that I do not pretend to understand. Like Dolly, I have my questions. How does God answer prayer? How do my prayers for another person affect that person? Why should I be telling God something God already knows? Why do some prayers seem to be answered while others are ignored? In the final analysis, prayer can be a puzzle.

Yet almost every human being, at some time or another, cries out to God in prayer. Prayer is a partnership to be established more than a puzzle to be solved. The ways of God are not our ways, and my mind is much too small to fully understand the mind of God. So I pray because God invites me into that kind of friendship.

Dear God, thank you for your invitation to pray,
for your invitation to friendship.
May we always be open to that invitation
and so pray with great faith in your love for us. Amen.

Dialogue with the Divine

Author Barbara Bartocci has a new book suggesting 101 ways for busy people to pray. Some of her suggestions are these:

1) "Give an alarm clock 'Alleluia'" when your alarm clock goes off. Mentally commit to living in gratitude for the day.
2) "Practice Shower Power. As you soap and rinse… pray to be cleansed from any feelings of anger, resentment, bitterness, or regret."
3) "Make a red-light act of contrition." Use the stoplights on the highway as a call to prayer. Talk with God instead of racing your motor.
4) Do "nighttime taps." When you go to bed, offer thanks for the day, pray for what you hope will come to pass, and ask forgiveness for the wrongs of the day. Rest. Sleep well.

Most Americans pray, even though few feel they pray enough or very effectively. Prayer is not a formula. Prayer is dialogue with the Divine. Prayer is like meeting a good friend for lunch. You enjoy each other's company, hold one another accountable, and support one another through the struggles of life.

O God, you are always ready to listen to us.
Help us to interrupt our busyness to talk with you
and to listen to you, for we need your support
and your grace in our lives. Amen.

Asking and Action

When it comes to prayer, have you learned to walk the walk as well as talk the talk? Prayer is action as well as asking. If I pray for my daily bread, am I willing to work to see that others are fed? If I ask God for forgiveness, am I willing to forgive others? If I pray for peace, will I live for peace? If I ask for the kingdom of God to come on earth as it is in heaven, am I willing to live by kingdom values?

It is one thing to wish, but quite another to engage in the work that empowers our wishes to come true. Maybe our prayers fall flat not because God is impotent, but because we are hesitant to support our prayers with our deepest devotion.

So, let us find a better way. The things, Lord, we pray for, give us the courage to work for. Let the desires of our hearts become the passions of our lives. Let our prayers empower us for action.

*O God, may we work with your Holy Spirit
in the world so that our prayers become
passions according to your will.
Empower us for action. Amen.*

For Others

A quiet and devout woman explained her devotional habits this way:

> *"I take the newspaper to bed with me and read the front page to find out what is going on in the world. For a little while, I pray about that. Then I read all the birth announcements, and I pray for these babies that are born and for their parents who have the awesome responsibility of raising a family. Finally I read the death notices. I think about these families whose hearts are broken at the loss of a loved one. I pray for them to be comforted. And then I go to sleep."*

The polls constantly remind us that almost everyone prays at some time in some way. Prayers can be simple pleas for help or lists of things that we need God to do. Someone said prayer in public schools will cease when teachers stop giving tests. I suspect they are right. Prayers reach a new level when we learn to pray for others as well as ourselves. To pray is to start a wave of goodness in the worst of circumstances. To pray is to tap into a power on high for the needs of the day. Prayer may not change things. Prayer always changes us.

*Dear Lord, let us never cease to pray to you.
Help us to remember that, even if we don't
see prayer changing things, we can know that
prayer is changing us. Amen.*

Unanswered Prayer

Did you hear about the boy who decided that prayer was just not worth it anymore? When his mother probed into the child's crisis of faith, she received this explanation: "I prayed and prayed for a new puppy dog. Instead, you and Daddy brought home a baby brother."

Well, I've had a few prayers that didn't turn out the way I expected either. How about you? Sometimes the requests were things I really didn't need and found myself better off without. In times like that, we can even thank God for unanswered prayers.

But that's not always the case. I've prayed for parents to live when it was obvious that their children needed them. I've pled for families to stay together who had great potential to contribute to society. Employment opportunities have a way of being manipulated by people with mixed motives.

So why pray, when it seems that God is unable to bring about the best, the fair, the right? I have one answer to that question. Prayer is not a matter of control. Prayer is a matter of communion. When things don't go just right, I need the company of God more than ever.

*O Lord, help us pray without ceasing
and then willingly and faithfully give
matters over to your control. We are
thankful for the gift of communion with you. Amen.*

World Crisis

It is not good for people to have spare time on their hands. As I lay in the hospital recently, flipping the channels on the TV, watching one newscast after another show bombings in the Middle East and more terrorist attacks in Baghdad, it all started to get to me. I found myself restless, anxious, feeling this is just too much to handle considering my physical condition. As I took my concern to God in prayer, he replied quite bluntly. "Why don't you turn it off? The remote is in your hand. You don't have to watch." Oh, that all of life's solutions were that simple.

The ordinary response to our war-torn world is to turn on the radio, open the newspaper, or talk to more people at the coffee shop about world situations. I believe in being informed, but how much information can we stand?

Maybe there is another approach to the troubles of the world. Maybe we need to get still, be quiet, step back, and listen for the voice of God instead of the babblings of talk-show hosts. It could help us gain a new perspective.

*Dear God, there is so much trouble in your world.
When we lose hope or feel tempted to add to problems by
engaging in divisiveness, help us to listen for your wisdom.
May our prayers be for the well-being of the whole world. Amen.*

Purpose

Making a Life

Author David Myers makes this observation: "We have express coffee, the World Wide Web, sport utility vehicles, and caller ID. We also have more depression, more fragile relationships, less community, and more suicidal teens than ever before. We know how to make a living, but do we know how to make a life?"

Well, do we know how to live? When everything you have ever wanted is not enough, what do you do? The rich and the powerful know something that the rest of us have yet to discover. They know that money, power, prestige, and fame do not satisfy that unnamable hunger of the soul. Life is not a matter of things. Life is a matter of relationships. Life is not a matter of power. Life is a matter of purpose. We have good reasons to be born save to consume the corn, eat the fish, and leave behind a dirty dish. There are eternal dimensions to our living and universal reasons for our existence. So, decide now to live, not merely survive. Invest in things that will out live you and make a difference in the light of eternity.

O God, we pray in the words of the apostle Paul.
May we be strengthened in our inner being with power,
that Christ may dwell in our hearts through faith
and that we may be rooted and grounded in love. Amen.

Creation

A visit to the zoo left me pondering the wide variety of God's good creation. Was God joking when he made the giraffe? Does that monkey really look like me? Do humpbacked camels have any reason to be? A little research informed me that camels were once called the "ships of the desert." These shaggy, awkward, stiff-legged, goose-necked beasts served a unique purpose for ancient travelers. Among their unusual features are these: Their nostril slits can be closed during sandstorms to keep the sand out. Their eyes are specifically designed to see for long distances. Their broad-toed feet won't sink in the sand. Clearly, the camel was made for the desert.

How are you uniquely and wonderfully made? If God can make the beasts of the field and the birds of the air for a particular purpose, don't you think he has some purpose for you? As your fingerprints and DNA are unique, so is your personhood. You have a reason to be born, a place to be useful, a contribution to make to the good of humanity. Find it and live it.

*Dear Creator God, you made us in your image to live
fully and faithfully according to your will.
Help us bring good to the world and to love others. Amen.*

Come Out of Hiding

You probably know Ted Giannoulas even though you do not recognize his name. Ted has been the San Diego Chicken for thirty years. "I have loved this alter ego," says Ted. "I discovered an untapped personality in that suit, making people laugh and stirring up the crowds at ball games." But lately Ted has been having second thoughts.

"You can lose yourself in that suit," laments Ted. "I have plenty of chicken stories, but I don't have any Ted stories."

I suspect there are a lot of people who feel like Ted Giannoulas. We have put on a costume, assumed a role, played a part in an effort to make a living, and lost ourselves in the process. People know us by what we do and not for who we are. We are children, parents, teachers, lawyers, clerks, construction workers. But who are we really? Who is the real person inside that suit? What are your hopes, your dreams and aspirations?

Isn't it about time you came out of your hiding? God created you to be you and me to be me. So, by God's grace, let's become our real selves.

*O Lord, you have searched us and known us.
Our masks and costumes cannot hide us from you.
Help us to know our true selves and to be those people
before you and before the people in our lives. Amen.*

If

The biggest little word in the English language may be that persistent little word "if." Rudyard Kipling surely thought so when he wrote:

> "If you can keep your head when all about you are losing theirs and blaming it on you;
> If you can trust yourself when all men doubt you, but make allowances for their doubting too…
> If you can dream—and not make dreams your master;
> If you can think—and not make thoughts your aim,
> If you can meet with Triumph and Disaster and treat those two imposters just the same…"

Ah, that's the stuff that adulthood is made of.

When things go bad, when trouble comes, when some tragedy plays havoc with our ordered lives, I am prone to lament: "Life has an 'if' right in the middle of it." Indeed it does. But that little word "if" has its possibilities too—if I can get an education, if I can endure this suffering, if I can seize this opportunity—who knows what I might be able to do?

So, here's the point. The world waits to see what you and I will do with the "ifs" of our lives.

Dear God, may we make the most of the many "ifs"
we are presented with throughout our lives.
Help us to see each if as an opportunity
to serve and glorify you. Amen.

Using What You Have

Homer and Mary Lou were courting on the front porch swing. Homer was deeply in love with Mary Lou. But he was also extremely shy. So Homer tried to increase his courage by saying, "Mary Lou, if I had a thousand eyes, they would all be looking at you. And Mary Lou, if I had a thousand arms, they would all be hugging you. And Mary Lou, if I had a thousand lips, they would all be kissing you."

Mary Lou stared Homer in the eye for a while and finally replied, "Homer, why don't you stop complaining about what you don't have and start using what you do have?"

I have a feeling most of us could use a little of Mary Lou's advice. We like to complain about our deficiencies instead of using our assets. If we had more money, we would be more generous. If we had more time, we would be more helpful. If we had more talent, we would do more good. Meanwhile, the Maker of us all must be wondering, "Why don't you use what you've got?" We all have something to share. We all have talents to use. We all have the capacity to care. Use it before you lose it.

You have given us many abilities, dear God.
Help us to recognize those abilities
and to seek ways to use them
for the good of those around us
and for the good of your world. Amen.

Types of People

Somebody said there are three types of people who populate the earth. There are people who make things happen. There are people who watch things happen. There are people who have no idea what is happening. What kind of person are you?

It's one thing to curse the darkness. It's another thing to light a candle. It's one thing to deplore evil. It's another thing to work for good. It's one thing to fix our minds on the horrible things humans are capable of doing to each other. It's something else to set our sights on lofty places.

The really great people of the world have been willing to risk their lives to make things happen. Martin Luther King had a dream that touched the conscience of America. Jesus had the radical idea of loving our enemies. Nelson Mandela dedicated himself to ending apartheid in South Africa. Are you a spectator or a player? Are you a commentator or a convener? Do you make things happen? Watch things happen? Or just remain oblivious to all happenings?

*Dear God of beauty and truth,
help us to ask ourselves what we are willing to risk
for your kingdom and then to answer that question honestly.
May we be people who light a candle in the darkness. Amen.*

Self-Discovery

Eastern College sociology professor Tony Campolo tells about a student who came to see him and announced that he would not be returning to school for the next semester.

"I need to go find myself," asserted the student. "I'm tired of being the person my family, my friends, my church, my school expects me to be. I've got to peel away the layers to find me."

Campolo, who has a reputation for directness, said to the student, "What if you turn out to be an onion and you get all the layers peeled off and discover there is nothing left? What if you take that long, grueling journey into yourself and, when you get there, nobody's home?"

Campolo gives us all something to think about. Self is not an essence waiting to be discovered through philosophical introspection. Self is an essence waiting to be created through the commitments we make and the vows we take. So the next time you feel like running away to find yourself, you may want to consider a more fruitful solution to the stress.

Dear Parent God, we are your children;
you created us in your image.
Remind us of that when we think
we have lost who we are. Amen.

The Best Is Yet to Be

A number of years ago, the Chicago Parks and Recreation Department held a contest to determine the best young artist in the area. Paintings were submitted, and a panel of impartial judges made the final decision. Much to everyone's surprise, an eight-year-old boy won the contest.

With TV cameras recording the event, the mayor awarded the boy first prize. The boy responded by saying "Thank you sir, but that painting ain't my best one." The shocked mayor replied, "Son, if you don't mind me asking, where is your best one?" Undaunted, the kid brushed the hair out of his eyes, threw back his shoulders, and said, "Sir, my best one ain't been drawn yet!"

I like the attitude of that kid—don't you? Certainly the best painting is yet to be painted, the best invention is yet to be invented, the best medicine is yet to be practiced. Those who believe the best is yet to be are on their way to accomplishing more than they imagine. For as the Scottish churchman and poet Horatius Bonar once said, "Let our reach exceed our grasp, or what's heaven for?"

*Dear God, may we strive to be and do our best,
not best according to the world's standards
but best according to your wisdom. Amen.*

Find Your Purpose

I can do anything. I can do nothing. I hear these two exaggerations all the time, don't you? Neither is true. I can't do everything. I can't sing. I can't build a house. I can't make a living playing golf. The list goes on. I am limited by my ability, my age, my opportunity. Some things are just out of reach for me, and I need to accept that.

Of course, the opposite is also false. People who think they can do nothing, accomplish nothing, produce nothing, or amount to nothing find themselves drowning in the muck of nothingness. Fear of failure keeps them from trying. Lack of self-confidence keeps them from succeeding.

There is a better way. You cannot do everything, but you can do something. You are a child of God. You have a purpose for being here. So find that purpose and pursue it with all your life.

Dear God, help us distinguish between what is impossible and what is possible through you. Help us to find our purposes and pursue them with all of our lives. Amen.

Gift of Love

Joe Ehrmann played professional football for the Baltimore Colts during the 1970s. There he became known as the "sack pack," the man who could mow others down on the field. But Joe Ehrmann learned a bigger purpose in life than knocking people down. He devoted his life after football to picking kids up.

As coach of the Gilman High School football team in Baltimore, Joe teaches kids to love and respect each other as the coaches love and respect them. As Joe puts it, "We are put on earth to love not hate, build up not tear down, to have fun not make people cry." And the Gilman High School football teams win state championships by playing up to that ideal.

Whether we are football players or fans in the stands, all of us hunger for love and respect. If we fail to get it at home, we will likely try to earn it in sports, through sex, or even by soaring to the top of our professions. But love cannot be earned. It is a gift to be received. That's why people like Joe Ehrmann make a difference.

Dear Jesus, you taught us to do unto others what we would have others do unto us. Help us to make a difference by loving and respecting others in your name. Amen.

Real Stars

Author and actor Ben Stein used to write a column about the rich and famous. Then on December 20, 2003, he quit. In his final article, Ben explained his departure this way:

> "Real stars are not riding around in the backs of limousines or in Porsches or getting trained in yoga or Pilates and eating raw fruit while they have Vietnamese girls do their nails… A real star, the kind who haunts my memory night and day, is the U.S. soldier in Baghdad who saw a little girl playing with a piece of unexploded ordnance on a street near where he was guarding a station. He pushed her aside and threw himself on it just as it exploded. He left a family desolate in California and a little girl alive in Baghdad."

A life that really matters is a life lived to help others. Life is not about our joy, our success, our recognition. Life is about being a devoted parent, a faithful spouse, a caring servant to those who depend on us day by day. Life is not a matter of getting. Life is a matter of giving. So if there is any good we can do, any help we can render, any difference we can make, let us not defer it or neglect it. Let us do it now, for we shall not pass this way again. No one stands taller than when they stoop to serve.

Your world is full of real stars all around us, O God.
Help us to recognize and support their work.
We know that real stars do your work with
courage, unselfishness, and humility.
May we be real stars too. Amen.

Life on a Conveyor Belt

Did you hear the story about the man at an airport who slipped and fell onto the conveyor belt when trying to retrieve his luggage? By the time he came to his senses, the conveyor was transporting him through the flaps into the darkness beyond.

At first he was frightened. Then he thought, I've been wanting to do this for years. Besides, this is probably not the time to get off.

So he rode the belt, still gripping his suitcase, until he and his bag passed through the flaps again into the light. That's when he found himself staring into the face of an official-looking woman who said, "You're not supposed to do that!" to which the man replied, "Have you ever tried it?"

"No!" bellowed the woman.

"Don't!" said the man as he swung his feet to the floor, tightened his grip on the suitcase handle, stood on the edge of the conveyor belt and walked off.

Do you ever feel like you're stuck on a conveyor belt, gripping your bag, with nowhere to get off? Life can be like that, can't it? In such times, we would do well to regain our perspective, renew our purpose, and move on.

Dear God help us to step off the conveyor belt we've allowed our lives to become. Only then will we be able to listen to you, examine our priorities, and set our purpose to live according to your will. Amen.

Between the Steps

Barbara Brown Taylor, professor of religion and spirituality, tells a story about a university professor who was invited to speak at a military base one December. The professor was met at the airport by an unforgettable soldier named Ralph. After the two introduced themselves to each other, they headed toward the baggage claim. But Ralph kept disappearing. He stopped once to help an older woman with her luggage. He stopped once to lift two toddlers up in the air to see Santa. He stopped again to give directions to someone who was lost.

Finally the professor said to Ralph, "Where did you learn that?"

"Where did I learn what?" replied Ralph.

"Where did you learn to live like that?" insisted the professor.

"During the war," said Ralph hesitantly. "I was in Vietnam. It was my job to clear mine fields. You never knew which step might be your last. So, I learned to live between the steps. And I guess I just never stopped."

If you lived as if each step were your last, what difference would it make for you? Would you be kinder, gentler, more anxious to help if you learned to live between the steps?

*O God of all of our days, help us to welcome
each day as an opportunity to love
and serve others. May we live
between the steps. Amen.*

Marking Time

A rocking chair can put you to sleep, but don't depend on its motion to get you anywhere. Have you thought about that? My wife and I recently bought each other rocking lounge chairs. They are the deluxe models with heat and massage and pulsations of every kind. Our idea of fun has evolved over time. While our chairs bring us the greatest of comfort and the finest of ease, they don't really get us anywhere. We can rock the night away and wind up right where we started.

While rest is essential and relaxation is helpful, too much rocking will leave you snoring instead of soaring. The monotony of routines, the monotony of daily duties, and the sameness of experience can have us going through the motions without making any difference. We were not put on earth to mark time. We were put here to make a difference—to see a wrong and try to right it, to observe a problem and try to solve it, to find a hurt and try to heal it. That takes effort, energy, and lots of hard work.

*Dear God who acts in the world, may we
work with you to help bring good in the world.
Thank you for opportunities to rest,
but nudge us when we've rested long. Amen.*

Fitting In

As author Robert Fulghum tells the story, "I was stuck in a church fellowship hall with eighty elementary students when I decided to entertain them with a little game of Giants, Wizards, and Dwarfs—a game that has no redemptive quality except to have children run around in a noisy frenzy until no one knows who wins and who loses.

"At the height of the confusion, I announced that it was time to decide if you are a giant, a wizard, or a dwarf. The words were hardly out of my mouth when a little girl tugged on my pants asking, 'Where do the mermaids stand?'

"'There are no mermaids in this game,' I replied.

"But the little girl insisted 'I'm a mermaid. Where do I stand?' With that I took her by the hand and let her stand by me, the newly announced captain of the sea."

Where do the mermaids stand? What do we do with people who fail to fit our pigeonholes, our norms, our available boxes? Answer that question and you can build a school, a church, a nation, a world. Some of the most creative contributors to society fail to fit our preconceived notions. But where would we be without them?

Creator God, you made all of us in your image and gave each of us different gifts. May we accept those who seem too different from us, remembering that these children of yours have gifts to share. Amen.

Time
(Or Patient Waiting)

Creative Pause

As I watched the ballroom-dancing competition on television recently, I was impressed by the dancers' timing as well as their movements. They knew when to go and when to stop. They knew how to soar high and when to sweep low. They knew how to pause gracefully at the completion of one movement before the beginning of another. Pause as well as participation made them good dancers.

Perhaps creative pauses are necessary in the dance of life too. In our hectic, hurry-up world, we are tempted to surge forward from one responsibility to another, failing even to catch our breath in between. We have places to go, things to do, a life to live. Rushing to the next assignment, we tend to forget that pausing is a part of living too.

So the next time you are in between, try something different. Instead of pulling harder, tugging quicker, pounding endlessly, pause, wait, and stay suspended. Let God lead you into grace-filled, purposeful movements of life. If we wait in confidence, the road ahead will become clear, and we will be refreshed for the journey.

*Dear God of the still, small voice, help us
to use the in-between times in our lives
as a chance to refresh ourselves in your presence
and to gain clarity for the days ahead. Amen.*

Puzzle

A rainy day at a retreat house inspired our family to tackle a jigsaw puzzle. Each of us had other things we would rather be doing, but since the rain prohibited golfing, swimming, fishing, or outdoor activity of any kind, we settled down to make a picture from a thousand pieces.

As we worked on this puzzle one piece at a time, here are some thoughts about life that came to my mind. 1) People seldom settle down to put the pieces together. That puzzle had been in the closet for a long, long time. 2) Each knobby piece with its protruding edge and unique shape fit into the whole. 3) It's harder to get the pieces to fit than it first appears. 4) Puzzles are solved more easily if the finished picture is on the box.

Our family completed the puzzle. Cheers and laughter came from the table when the last piece was put in its place. And I walked away with some lessons for the bigger puzzle of life. So how about it? Are you taking the time to find the ways the knobby pieces of your life fit together?

*Dear God, sometimes life seems like
a 1,000-piece puzzle with no picture on the box.
But you gave us the ultimate picture when
you sent us Jesus to show us how to love and serve.
May we take the time to find your will for our lives. Amen.*

Slow Down

Bestselling writer Barbara Johnson said, "Patience is the ability to idle your motor when you feel like stripping your gears." If you happen to be in a traffic jam right now, what a perfect place to practice patience! There the rubber of good intention hits the road of reality. You're already late for work. The pressure is on. Then, sure enough, you're stopped for the third time trying to get through the light at a construction site. We've all been there. What do you do? Race your motor? Blow your horn? Mouth profanities to construction crews? Ask God to give you patience and give it now?

Maybe there is a better way. Slow down your emotions along with your motor. Come to understand that nobody gets to where they are going by blowing their horns. Ask the Lord to help you keep your cool. And best of all, determine now to plan for interruptions and delays in the course of your day. It could make all the difference.

O God, how patient you are with us. Teach us patience,
that in times of waiting we may not miss
an important word from you.
Help us keep our cool. Amen.

Give Yourself a Break Today

"Give yourself a break today!" Have you the power to do that? We must learn to be as patient with ourselves as God is with us. For perfectionists, that's a tall order. Many of us expect to get it right the first time every time. We want to be perfect and to be perfect now. The hand that holds the whip over ourselves is most often our own.

Since perfectionism is a problem more than a promise, why not give yourself a break today? The God who foreordained delete keys for computers and forgiveness as the heart of prayer is more anxious to accept you as you are than you are likely to accept yourself. Certainly people need to establish boundaries and pursue goals. We also need to establish realistic expectations and celebrate imperfect successes. So be responsible, but not overly responsible. Be compassionate, but not compulsive. Be dependable, but not obsessive. Give yourself a break today.

O God of perfect love, forgive us for striving to be perfect,
for perfection belongs only to you.
May we always seek your guidance so that we may be
the faithful disciples you want us to be. Amen.

Life Stages

A boy was thumbing through a family photo album when he discovered a portrait of a curly headed, muscular gentleman. "Who's that?" inquired the boy.

"That's your father," came the reply.

"Then whose that baldheaded, potbellied man who lives with us now?" asked the boy. "I thought he was my father."

Time like an ever rolling stream does take its toll. We bulge. We change. We grow older. We are no longer what we once were. And who knows what we shall yet become? But believe it or not, I kind of like it that way.

No, I don't enjoy the pains of aging, but I do enjoy the peace of maturity. People may not be impressed with how I look, but I am more comfortable with who I am. I may not be as healthy as I once was, but I am as full of life as I ever was. Time has its liabilities. Time, also, has its assets.

So, let us embrace each stage of life as a gift from God.

O life-giving God, may each of us view where we are in our lives right now—no matter what stage— as a truly beneficent gift from you and be grateful. Amen.

Time

Carl Sandburg once said, "Time is the coin of your life. It is the only coin."

How are you spending the time of your life? Time management experts tell us the average American in a lifetime spends five years waiting in line and six months waiting at traffic lights. We also spend one year searching for misplaced objects, six years eating, eight months opening junk mail, and two years trying to return telephone calls.

By contrast, the average married couple spends four minutes a day in meaningful conversation with each other and 30 seconds a day in dialogue with their children.

The days of our lives are 24 hours, 440 minutes, 86,400 seconds, nothing more, nothing less. Time is a precious, divine gift. The use of time is a sacred responsibility. How we spend what we've got—well, that's what life is made of.

*Dear God of eternity, help us to be
faithful in our use of time you have given us.
May we use our time to love others,
to do justice, and to walk humbly with you. Amen.*

 *Make it a good day.*

www.ingramcontent.com/pod-product-compliance
Lightning Source LLC
Chambersburg PA
CBHW022105040426
42451CB00007B/134